THE CULT OF PERFECTION

Making Peace
With Your
Inner Overachiever

Cooper Lawrence

Guilford, Connecticut
An imprint of The Globe Pequot Press

To buy books in quantity for corporate use
or incentives, call **(800) 962–0973,**
or e-mail **premiums@GlobePequot.com.**

 skirt!® is an attitude . . . spirited, independent, outspoken, serious, playful and irreverent, sometimes controversial, always passionate.

skirt!® is an imprint of The Globe Pequot Press.

skirt!® is a registered trademark of Morris Publishing Group, LLC, and is used with express permission.

10 9 8 7 6 5 4 3 2

Printed in the United States of America

Library of Congress Cataloging-in-Publication Data

Lawrence, Cooper.
  The cult of perfection : making peace with your inner overachiever / Cooper Lawrence.
      p. cm.
ISBN: 978-1-59921-179-4
  1. Overachievement. 2. Quality of life. 3. Women—Conduct of life. I. Title.

BF637.O94L39 2008
158.1—dc22

2007007699

For Sandi,
my mother and role model

Contents

# Introduction

I'm thinking of lobbying for yet another federal reform of daylight saving time. Bringing it forward from April to March just wasn't enough: I need more time in my day. In fact, I would like to change the clocks altogether—but just for us overachieving women who sure could use a few more hours. And you know what? I'd like the makeup counters and shoe departments at retail chains to do their bit, too, and start staying open much later.

I have been an overachiever my whole life. I started working in radio more than twelve years ago, and my very first radio job says it all. I was a deejay on the overnight shift (midnight until 6:00 a.m.) and did weekend shifts, too, but I also drove the station's promotional van, made several appearances a week at bars and clubs and store openings to promote the station and hand out T-shirts, and wrote, produced, and voiced many of the commercials that were heard on the station. I worked an average of 60 hours a week, some weeks more than that.

The next stage of my career was just as busy. I was a traffic and news reporter on morning radio in New York (the number-one radio market); I went to school during the day to receive my master's degree in Applied Developmental Psychology; and at night I produced a second radio show.

Now that I finally have my own radio show (aptly named the *Cooper Lawrence Show*), nothing has changed. A day in my life looks

> Whole forests of books and articles have been written about people like us, telling us that we do too much, and that we need to stop. Well, I am here to tell you that I'm not stopping anytime soon.

like this: I spend time finishing my PhD and writing my next book, make regular TV appearances, and fit in meetings with radio and TV producers. Producers are people who make things happen, and I have many of them in my life to make *it* happen—several for my radio show, several more for TV appearances—and I meet with all of them each day to plan what I will be doing. Running over to Headline News's *Showbiz Tonight* or another TV outlet to do a segment about the latest celebrity breakup, or to give the psychological spin on why young Hollywood celebs act the way they do, is a normal part of my day. Then I hop a train or jump in a cab to get over to my radio studio. I am on every weeknight doing a talk radio show for three hours, from 7:00 until 10:00 p.m. Then I leave work and, after a quick snack, I get back to writing. I like to kid myself that in the midst of everything else I get to the gym four or five times a week, but some weeks I only make it twice. Luckily my husband has the kind of career where he is around most days, so we do spend a great deal of time together. In my free time I answer all of the e-mail and MySpace messages I get for the radio show, manage a manicure every now and then, see my friends, fit in a column once in a while at *CosmoGIRL!* . . . and you know what? I *love* every second of it; I would not trade my life for anything.

If you've picked up this book, chances are your calendar is as busy as mine, perhaps even busier. Whole forests of books and articles have been written about people like us, telling us that we do too much and that we need to stop. Well, I am here to tell you that I'm not stopping anytime soon. I don't have kids, so your day is way busier if you do. I am here to tell you that I am in fact offended when psychologists write that being an overachiever is unhealthy, and fail to acknowledge its positive aspects. For many of us it's a fulfilling way of life—it's what makes us happy, and more important, it's what makes us . . . us. Psychologists who see only problems in our overachieving lifestyle clearly don't know the joy it can bring us. I challenge them to take a less biased look at overachievers: They will see how well many of our lives have turned out, and how satisfying our feelings of accomplishment can be.

The aim of this book is not to tame you or "cure" you of your overachieving impulses. The aim is to give you the tools you need so that your overachieving personality works for you. I am not going to deny that we overachievers face certain challenges: At times it can be stressful and anxiety-inducing to live up to our own high expectations. Sometimes our schedule is so crammed that it feels like things are slipping out of our grasp, or that we're losing touch with our family and friends. And even the

> The aim of this book is not to tame you or "cure" you of your overachieving impulses. The aim is to give you the tools you need so that your overachieving personality works for you.

most confident overachieving woman has her moments of self-doubt. I will give you practical advice on overcoming these challenges. I will show you how to monitor and ease your stress; manage your time and prioritize your tasks so you don't feel overwhelmed; build real and lasting self-esteem; and always be the one in control. The goal: To be *at peace* with your inner overachiever.

What you will also get from this book is a better understanding of yourself as an overachiever. What made you this way? Were you born to be an overachiever, or was it how your parents raised you? What motivates you and helps you achieve your goals? And what upsets your equilibrium and makes you feel like you're losing your grip? I'll help you find the answers to all these questions.

In writing this book I interviewed countless overachieving women, who were wonderfully candid about the challenges, hardships, and setbacks they've faced in life, and how they've overcome them. They opened up about what motivates them, what works for them, and what they love about their lives. Reading their stories, you will come to see that you are not alone.

Indeed, you are one of a growing band of women whose calendars are overflowing with appointments and whose résumés make the Yellow Pages look like a pamphlet. We don't chant or wear brightly colored robes or have pictures around our necks of a guru we've never met, but, like a cult, we all share a devotion to the same thing: the quest for perfection. Think of us as a club, or a sorority—a sisterhood of women all striving to be the best at whatever we have chosen to be in life. "Perfection," as we see it, is a state of unsurpassed excellence, and that is the goal of all overachievers. We aim for excellence; we aim to reach the peak of achievement; we aim to be the best in every facet of our lives.

How to Use This Book

Okay, if you are holding this book in one hand while you're checking your messages on your BlackBerry with your other hand and have been turning pages with your nose (oh, hold on, is that a cradle you're rocking with your foot?), then raise your . . . other foot. This book is designed with the overachiever in mind: It's ideal to read it from beginning to end, but if you're reading on the run, I understand that you might prefer to pick out certain topics at your own pace. That's why there are lots of bold headings and boxes—that way you can find information quickly and easily.

If you want to focus on the nitty-gritty, practical solutions to the challenges we overachievers face, go straight to the boxes headed **To Do.** If reading about the experiences of other overachieving women is your main interest, then look for the boxes headed **Tales from the Treadmill.**

Turn to Part 1 for the lowdown on what we mean by the word *overachiever* and for help identifying your own inner overachiever. In Part 2 we look at the impact that being an overachiever has on your home life, your relationships with your friends, your health and state of mind, and your future. In each chapter in Part 2 you will find the headings **The Good, The Bad,** and **The Better. The Good** refers to the positive impacts of overachieving and **The Bad** to the potentially negative impacts. **The Better** is my advice on how to maximize the good and minimize the bad so that you are at peace with your inner overachiever.

In **The Types,** I outline familiar stereotypes of overachieving women. If you recognize a little bit of yourself in any of these women, don't take it too much to heart: I'm having a gentle dig at the slightly nutty behavior we overachievers can indulge in from time to time. (Believe me, I do include myself in this.) In Part 2 you'll also find inspiring stories of great women in history who have shown how much good we overachievers can do for the world: Look for the boxes headed **The Lives of History's Classic Overachievers.**

Part 3 is all about learning to understand yourself and what helped to make you an overachieving woman: the personality you were born with, how you were raised, your self-image and belief in what you can achieve, major life events, and even your economic and social circumstances. You'll find plenty of advice to help you deal with issues you may be struggling with from your childhood; maintain a healthy sense of self-esteem; turn negative life events into opportunities to build something positive; and handle economic and social pressures. While Part 3 focuses on the factors that led you to become an overachiever, don't lose sight of the fact that *you* are the one in control of your life. For the final word on how to make sure you always keep hold of the reins, look for the heading **You're in Control** at the end of each chapter in Part 3.

Now, let's get started. First off, what exactly *is* an overachiever?

1

What Is an Overachiever?

If you strive for excellence in every part of your life, and give everything to the career or role you have chosen for yourself, you are most certainly an overachiever.

Chapter One

Defining
"Overachiever"

The world wants winners. Confident, successful, intelligent, self-assured winners who are at the top of their game.

The world will root for you to be the best you can be—but that's not enough if you are an overachiever. You want to fulfill that wish, and then some. And your overachieving best friend? She always has an ear to lend, a cough drop as soon as she hears you clear your throat, and a small container of hand sanitizer in case you want to eat your sandwich and are nowhere near a sink to wash up. She likes to show the world that she has perfect children, a fabulous husband to father them, a successful career, a perfect lawn, and soft, manageable hair—all while still being a great friend to you. Overachieving is the new feminism—or the new black, I can't remember which one.

If you *are* that overachieving friend, you judge yourself on a higher level than you judge everyone else. It's okay for your friends to get 85s on their exams, marry halfway decent men, and bowl a 54—but it's not okay for you. The parameters of how far you can go, how far you can stretch yourself, are limitless.

As women, we have more opportunities now than at any other time in history, and that means that we also have more choices to make than ever before. There are so many things we can achieve, so many people we can be. This vast array of life choices can be confusing and overwhelming for the regular person, but not for you as an overachiever: You choose all of them. You *have to* have everything at once: a stellar career, a contented husband, cherubic children, your own blog, a mastery of Ashtanga yoga, the ability to serve your family gourmet meals in thirty minutes or less, an MBA, a novel you're working on, spiritual enlightenment, perfectly coiffed hair, and a stock portfolio others envy.

What sets you apart from other women is your *drive*. While others may be content with an average level of performance and achievement, you are driven to reach higher, to exceed your own and everyone else's expectations. If you're a schoolteacher, you study for further qualifications and take on extra tasks at school; you work your way up, with the principal's office in mind. If you're a doctor, you don't stop at getting a position in your local family practice; you work hard to be the best doctor there, until you're running not just that practice but a chain of them. If you're a stay-at-home mom, you don't just keep your household running; you run the cleanest, happiest, healthiest, most organized household on your block. And no matter whether you are a career woman or work at home looking after your family, you still manage to achieve a million other things: You work on your health and fitness, always seem to be studying something, or have more interests, hobbies, and charitable causes than anyone you know.

Maybe the best way to define an overachiever is by talking about what she *isn't*. For instance, if you are naturally smart, if you applied yourself in school and as a result did well and now have a good career—let's say you're a doctor—you may not be an overachiever. If you inherited a job from your family and now run a large part of the family business—not an overachiever. (Making partner at your law firm at twenty-eight by sleeping with your boss also doesn't make you an overachiever—it does, however, make you annoying.)

To the outside world it might seem that as an overachiever you "have it all." What they don't realize is that you are never fully satisfied with what you've got right now, because you can see how much *more* you can achieve. Each day you want to do even better than the day before. Your goals are always growing and changing. The only thing that remains constant is your motivation to reach them. Your career is good, just not good *enough* yet. Recognition from your peers? Meh! A good salary and underlings nipping at your heels to get where you are? It's okay . . . but only *just*. The same goes for your home, car, fitness level, educational qualifications. What you have at present may seem great to others, and, indeed, you're aware of that—but your overachieving abilities need to be constantly challenged and tested by new, different goals. You feel like you're just getting started.

Just to be clear, when we say *overachiever* we're talking about someone for whom success is not enough. As an overachiever you have to be better at your job than everyone else; you have to be the ideal worker or boss; you want to be fitter, younger looking, better dressed. You have to be the best at everything you choose to do, all at the same time. (You might not *be* the best at the moment, but make no mistake, that is your goal.)

Sometimes an overachiever excels in every area of her life except the one she really wants to excel in. You know the type—you may even be one of these women. You have worked extremely hard on certain things and succeeded beyond anyone's wildest dreams. Perhaps you were made the CEO of a major company before you

Tales from the Treadmill: Alexandra

Alexandra is myopic when it comes to her job as a corporate lawyer. She admits that her focus started early: "The top twenty-five schools have an admission rate of only about 10 percent; consequently I knew that how I spent my summers was going to be pivotal in becoming one of the lucky few." Once she made it to law school, Alexandra obtained special permission from the dean to take more classes than the standard course load each semester. She excelled in them all, maintained an outstanding GPA as well as an editorship of the law review, and took business classes on the side. Alexandra admitted to me that she considered going for her MBA after graduating from law school, but a job offer from a prestigious firm swayed her. Yet for all of Alexandra's accomplishments, her Ivy League education, and her six-figure salary, she is unable to settle on turned thirty, or became the first woman to run a particular division of a global organization—yet your love life is nonexistent. That's the one area of your life that you haven't been able to make headway in, even though you have the motivation. Being solo at the company Christmas party or at your best friend's wedding is less a reminder about your lack of romance than it is the fact there's one area of your life you cannot control. One area in which you have not yet achieved, much less overachieved. You are without what you consider to be the "perfect mate." Even this is a sign that you are an overachiever: Your criteria for the ideal partner are much stricter

a man. "My standards are too high, I know that. I meet men all the time and never feel that they are what I am looking for."

This causes Alexandra a great deal of anxiety, and she finds herself questioning her choices every once in a while. She now sees that she was so determined to do and be and accomplish that she never stopped to think that the kind of person she was becoming might intimidate the kinds of men she was interested in. Alexandra also realizes that the more she has learned, the more she knows—and there's a side to her that believes the old adage "Ignorance is bliss." She wishes, at times, for a simpler life. She wishes that she didn't want so many things, want to be so many things, want to accomplish so much. Now that she is on the corporate treadmill, getting off would be career suicide. She says, "You can't get as far as I have, especially as a woman, and then take a few years off to peruse the Maldives or search your soul, or even have children, and then expect to return and be back on top, or at least where you left off."

> You can't just be a mom; you must be Supermom, a moniker donned by nobody in the real world, just fabricated by the press, yet you have bought in, hook, line, and sinker.

than they were before you were fabulous. Now your other half needs to be not only worthy of you, but better than you. After all, you will pass an equal pretty quickly on your journey upward; you'll need someone superior to keep you on those well-pedicured toes.

Maybe you became the ultimate wife and mother, and you spend your days making sure everything looks perfect on the outside—happy husband, happy kids who are regularly shuttled, play-dated, and bathed, working on their own little résumés—but inside you wonder whatever happened to your dreams. Could you still become a rock star or be on the Forbes 200 Best Small Companies list as well? Could you fit it all in? You think so. While being the perfect wife and mother, you are also on every board known to man, have started a campaign at your kids' school for healthier lunches, are taking tennis lessons, and belong to three book clubs. Your life is almost as overscheduled as your kids'. You can't just be a mom; you must be Supermom, a moniker donned by nobody in the real world, just fabricated by the press, yet you have bought in, hook, line, and sinker. Heaven forbid if someone accuses you of not being a great mother. Some "Supermoms" are so focused on doing and being and achieving for their families that they don't even realize they're driving their families nuts in the process.

Tales from the Treadmill: Mary Beth

Mary Beth set out to be a better mother than her mother was, and to set a great example for her children. Not only was it important for her to be active in her community, she also strove for her kids to be involved. Her cause? Making the schools in her area drug-free. She read an article in the paper about the prevalence of drug use amongst teens, and the efforts of a group of mothers in another town to fix the problem. Inspired, she began researching drug education programs and talking to local law enforcement officers. She started gathering the troops: other mothers whose time she could usurp for her cause. This added to her list of daily to-do's, which included at least forty minutes on her cross trainer, half an hour of weight training, and at least an hour writing her novel—the one she has sworn to finish by Labor Day, after she re-landscapes the front yard. (She has found a combination of birch and Japanese maple trees that will look just perfect!) Are you exhausted reading everything on Mary Beth's list? Yeah, so am I, but now you get the picture.

Are You an Overachiever?

Studies have shown that one out of every six women is an overachiever, so if you're looking around the room at your five closest friends, thinking they're all slackers, then the overachiever is you. Being an overachiever is a lot like being sixteen years old and finding out that there's no Santa Claus: You are always the last to know.

You've probably been building yourself into an overachiever all your life. In high school maybe you took advanced placement (AP) classes and were on several teams and/or clubs, not to mention all the other extracurricular stuff you did. Whether it was volunteering in your community, being on yet another sports team outside of school, taking acting classes at the local theater, or all of the above, you have been training to be an overachiever your whole life. Yet on one level, you never saw it coming.

Is This You?

When I have an idea, I:
- A. Talk about it endlessly and start strategizing how to make it happen.
- B. Think about it a lot but don't act on it as fast as I should.

My to-do list:
- A. Consists of two lists: one with my day-to-day chores, and another with all of my life goals. As I check off life goals, I revise that list and add new life goals.
- B. Contains only my day-to-day chores such as "Get milk" and "Stop at post office."

When it comes to deadlines:
- A. I get the work done ahead of time.
- B. I try to make my deadlines, but sometimes I have to extend them.

I feel overwhelmed:
- A. Most of the time.
- B. Almost never.

When a problem arises I:
- A. Tackle it immediately; it's one less thing on my plate.
- B. Only deal with it when I absolutely have to.

Here's what I mean. I had a few moments when I was in my early twenties that clued me in to the fact I might be an overachiever. The first one was more of a metaphor for my overachieving ways, and it took my best friend Wayne, who knew me better than anyone else, to help me see the light. We were walking through the streets of Manhattan, running some errands, and at each store we visited I picked up yet another item that I had to accommodate in my already overstuffed leather multi-functional tote. It never occurred to me that the bag

When my boss criticizes my work:
- A. I assume she knows best and is looking at the big picture, as I am, so I work even harder.
- B. It makes me feel terrible and I want to give up.

My achievements are:
- A. Pretty spectacular, but I know there's so much more I can do.
- B. For my benefit and I don't care if nobody else is impressed by them.

When I'm on vacation:
- A. It drives me nuts to sit around and do nothing; I'm terribly restless.
- B. I can let the world slip away and I can just zone out for weeks at a time.

When it comes to my family and friends:
- A. They need to understand that everything I'm doing is important to me; if they love me, they'll get that.
- B. They always come first, and if it means letting a project go, I will.

If I am the lead person on a project, I:
- A. Know it will get done and it will be done well.
- B. Wish someone else would take charge; it makes me really anxious to have that kind of pressure.

could not sustain its mass, and when it began to burst at the seams, I was truly surprised. I remember Wayne saying to me: "Of course you're surprised, this is how you are with everything. You fill up as much as you can handle, never seeing that you are inches away from ripping at the seams." If that wasn't enough of a harbinger of over-achieving to come, the following month my boyfriend of two years ended our relationship, telling me, "I don't know where I fit into your world. You don't just have a busy day, you have a busy *life!*" Hey, some people see the glass as half full—the overachiever sees

What Your Answers Say About You

Mostly As:

You, my friend, are most certainly an overachiever—as if you didn't already know that. You strive for excellence in every part of your life, and you give everything to the career or role you have chosen for yourself. And that is justified because, let's face it, it's hard enough being a woman regardless of what path you choose. If you are a mother, you are inherently overburdened. If you are a career gal, many industries are still such boys' clubs. So what's a girl to do but work hard at it, right?

Your dogged determination can be applied to any challenge that comes up in your life; you are ready to take on the world. But at times you feel besieged by it all and want to run screaming. The paradox is: Taking time out to come up for air causes you just as much anxiety. You feel that if you take your eye off the race for a second, you will lose your place at the head of the pack. You're damned if you do, damned if you don't. However, there are other options. First off, it's not a bad idea to let your coworkers, your significant other, and your friends wear some of the armor. Let them do their jobs; trust that they can handle them. Second, trust yourself. You are highly talented, uniquely motivated, and you are special. The

the glass as not being big enough to hold all the liquid she needs to put into it.

In general, overachievers strive to accomplish each and every goal they have set, yet along the way they are chronically plagued by self-doubt. You're probably very familiar with those moments when you ask yourself if you are doing the right thing or are good enough to achieve the goals you have set for yourself. That type of self-doubt can be pervasive, but it also helps keep overachievers motivated. While the overachiever may often be nagged by the voice of self-doubt, she

cream rises to the top, you don't always have to push it there. If you don't take "you" time, then not only will you eventually self-destruct, you will also miss out on all the good stuff in your peripheral vision along the way.

Mostly Bs:

You admit that maybe you could try harder if you were really motivated to, and that you don't always do your very best. And that is perfectly fine. Perhaps what you value in life is friends, family, and the time you spend with them. Perhaps you don't "get" the whole run-yourself-ragged thing. You just have different priorities than overachievers. An issue arises only when your attitudes become a justification for not trying harder, or not achieving everything you want to. Do you secretly wish that your life were better? Do you feel you have more to offer, and that if you felt better about yourself maybe you could be spectacular? If you envy your over-achieving sisters because they take control of their lives rather than let life happen to them—or worse, let others tell them who they are—then take a cue from this book. Check out what makes overachievers unique, and see whether the positive aspects of their lives can inspire change in your own life.

keeps going. I'll explore this in Chapter Nine, but suffice it to say: Self-doubt can influence the decision-making of a regular person, taking him or her down another road entirely—not us overachievers, though. We're warriors in this way.

Types of Overachievers

Most of us can trace the roots of our overachieving back to childhood and feel like we have an overachieving little girl trapped inside. Later on, I'll go into the many and varied causes and types of overachievement, but first I'd like to introduce you to three of the more powerful archetypes: the gifted girl who grew up with unrealistic expectations, the mediocre girl who strove to be seen as extraordinary, and the girl who did everything to try to impress her disapproving mother. Here they are now, all grown up, and still desperate for approval.

The "Gifted" Overachiever

As a gifted child, at a very young age you had high expectations put upon you, so you grew up pressured to be better, faster, stronger, smarter . . . to become Superwoman! Perhaps back in your school days you were taken out of your regular classroom and placed in one considered more nourishing. But alas, a simple change of environment has an impact on the way a girl perceives herself. You can view yourself a number of ways, especially in those early years when you're figuring out who you are and who you want to be—

the smart girl, the popular girl, the life of the party, the rebel, or someone else. The way you see yourself, and whether you feel positive or negative about yourself, is formed to some degree by your environment and the people around you. As a child, what impact did you have on the kids in your classroom, your teacher, and your family? And how did they perceive you? This all makes a difference when you reach the age when it's time to decide who you are and what you want out of life.

For example, one day you are in algebra class with everyone else, wondering what that smell is and whether it's coming from the boy in the front row, and then suddenly you are with all the smart kids in an honors class, away from your friends. You may perceive your academic self in a brand-new, positive light (*Hey, I'm smart!*) but see your social self in a negative light (*My friends hate smart*). Thus begins an imbalance you may carry for years to come.

Your newfound identity as a gifted child could work against you in other ways. In the regular class with the regular kids you were at the top of the class; now that you're in with the smart kids, you're at the bottom. To regain that top-of-the-class position, you need to work harder than ever before; you have to come up with a strategy to become better than the other kids. Thus begins your overachieving life.

Being gifted may also place expectations upon you that are greater than everyone else's your age, like higher career expectations. You say to yourself: *Well, I was all geared up to be a towel girl for the Seattle Supersonics, but now I have to go cure cancer.* You may be confused about who you ought to be versus who you thought you were.

Gifted girls are expected to be overachievers, but being gifted doesn't mean that you're equipped to make complex decisions about your life and your future. And there are many different ways a person can be gifted—perhaps as a girl you were a math genius, a virtuoso on the violin, a champion debater. In other words, there is no one way to be gifted, so for many gifted people there are no role models; they have to make up their own rules as they go along. This, plus being assigned the label of "gifted" at a young age, has an impact. Heck, it's difficult enough to grow up as it is; it's even harder when you're placed in special programs and pulled away from your peers. Adult things are now expected of you. Consequently, you begin to feel pressure, which you internalize. While you would like to conform and be like all of your friends, you aren't like them anymore; you are special in a good way and there are those demands to excel weighing you down. So guess what happens next. Come on, guess . . . you've got it: You're always afraid of making the wrong choice, so you either stop choosing to do things, or you do all of them.

It's a sick, sad way to live, and I can totally relate.

The Mediocre Girl

Next there is the mediocre girl. Early on this girl started overcompensating for her mediocrity—most likely academic—by piling on her plate more than humanly possible, quantity over quality. She might have been an average student, but her list of extracurricular activities was longer than the ole mighty Mississip'.

If you are an overachiever, mediocrity is something you will not tolerate. While your life may be ordinary at the moment, you are ever-so-aware that this state can change— and *will* change, if you have anything to do with it. The definition of what is mediocre is subjective, but to the overachiever it reads like "inadequate." It means that you are just not trying hard enough and have the potential to achieve so much more.

> We will not be seen as average, because inside we know that we are not. We can feel it: We are bound for greatness, and it's just a matter of time.

For many of us this started in school, where we heard continually that we were "not working to our full potential" or were "one of the brightest in the class, but she just doesn't apply herself." Okay, you want to see application? How about this, Mrs. Guidance Counselor: cheerleader, varsity softball team as a freshman, the debate team, theater club, yearbook committee, and volunteering on the weekends for Big Brothers, Big Sisters, all while starring in the local production of *Peter Pan*. Is that enough "application" for you?

Overachieving women have the "See, I told you so" gene that makes us need to be right even at the expense of our own sleep. We will not be seen as average, because inside we know that we are not. We can feel it: We are bound for greatness, and it's just a matter of time. At some point we read a book about greatness, or were inspired

Tales from the Treadmill: Jennifer

It's interesting that many classic overachieving women I interviewed didn't think that they fit into the category. You can judge this one for yourself.

Jennifer, who just turned thirty-two, has a PhD in Environmental Toxicology from a prominent university from which—of course—she graduated with honors. She has a plum job—a fellowship in Washington, D.C., for the Environmental Protection Agency (EPA)—and is planning her wedding to her fiancé, who holds a PhD in biology. She is planning to have two children, whose first seven years will be divided between Puerto Rico and New York. Jennifer explains that it is so her children can grow up bilingual, since those first years of brain growth are the most critical for language development.

Oh, and did I mention that at the start of our interview Jennifer asked why I would want to talk with her since she is in no way an overachiever?

Jennifer recalls, "In high school I had such a different experience than your typical high school student. I was in honors classes, but I was also a cheerleader." I asked Jennifer if those were her only two extracurricular activities in high school. She replied, "Oh no, I was in the science honors society, Amnesty, the swim team, and outside of school I took a photography class—oh, I was also on the gymnastics team, but nobody ever called me an overachiever." During her summers Jennifer went to performing-arts camp for photography and also for dance, which she admits she was not as good at. "I chose dance because you had to have a minor."

Some overachievers like Jennifer were conditioned to get straight As in school. I asked her why she had to get As, and whether she would have settled for Bs, to which she countered, "That's the wrong question. You should be asking me what were the best grades for me, because if a C student can only get Cs then that's okay for them, but I'm an A student so my best were As, and I was just doing my best. My parents are the driving force. I wasn't going to be half-assed about study. Why not do the best that I could do?" Did Jennifer ever get a C? I had to know.

"I did get a C once, and then never again, but it was because I did something stupid. When I first got to college I didn't know exactly what I wanted to do and in high school I loved physics class, so in college I signed up for calculus. I had taken pre-calc in high school, but all the other kids in the class were way ahead of me and this was their major. So I met with the professor for help three to four times a week. I think he gave me a C for trying. I don't beat myself up over it because I realized it's just not my strength, so I learned to play to my strengths and that never happened again. If I ever do something that is my strength and it doesn't go how I would like it to, I'm just frustrated, but I keep at it until I have succeeded. I don't know if I'm an overachiever, maybe just tenacious."

by a woman who made something out of nothing. We swear to the gods above that we will be great too, we will succeed. Mantras start streaming through our heads, and we begin to put them in our mental needlepoint—words of inspiration like "The world is full of rejection, it's that one success that you wait for" and other such untruths.

The Girl with the Disapproving Mother

Third, there is the girl with the disapproving mother who thought to herself: "Maybe if I do *this* she'll approve; What about *this*; How about *that*; What about *now*?" The overall message she received as a girl was: "Whatever you do, it will never be good enough."

The daughters of parents with a disapproving parenting style tend to have a poorer sense of self, and so as women we retaliate by doing our own little dog-and-pony show. You can just picture the barker at the tent. "Ladies and gentlemen, step right up to see how, defying all odds, this woman will balance on her nose: a new business; winning yet another award; a private jet; and being elected to local office—all before lunch! Ooooh, sorry . . . parents are not impressed. Better luck next time."

Kidnapping is on the rise, but not in the traditional sense—the new kidnappers are much more devious. In this kind of kidnapping, a mother holds her love ransom in exchange for her daughter marrying the perfect husband, having a secure career, and one day giving her grandchildren (not too soon, she doesn't want to feel old or be called "Grandma" yet . . . don't worry, she'll tell you when). It all begins when you are little and your mom starts to tell you how you should feel, act, think; what you should want, do, be, and wear. Lots of "shoulds," not a lot of guidance. Parenting like this can spring from several sources: jealousy, a mother's desire to control her daughter's life, or a mother's own fears projected onto her daughter.

Mom may feel that the world has been unkind to her and out of love for you she doesn't want you to face the same pain. As a result, she would prefer that you take the safe road: a nine-to-five job with a 401K plan, health and dental insurance, a short commute, and two weeks' vacation a year, which you will spend at an all-inclusive resort with the rest of the non-risk-takers. You will marry someone who loves you, even though you are not truly interested; your mother will remind you that you "could do worse." Then you will have 2.5 children, a dog, a cat, and two fish that you name "Gin" and "Tonic" as a harbinger of your impending alcohol problems. *Or* you will become an overachieving daughter who takes immeasurable risks because, let's face it, no risk, no reward.

When you have a disapproving mother, what you get is a daughter who heaps more and more on her résumé, because she thinks that if she becomes more impressive, maybe then her mother will approve, maybe then her mother will see that she is worth something, and worthy of her love. The sad truth here is . . . yeah . . . no, ain't gonna happen.

Perhaps you are the daughter who makes it easy for your mother to disapprove by choosing an esoteric career that she not only cannot relate to, but is also easy to criticize. You may want to be a painter, actress, or singer. The disapproving mother and the artistic or creatively inclined overachieving daughter are a volatile concoction. Scientists are still trying to figure out how that chemical reaction can be harnessed for energy, and one day they will—I can feel it in my overachieving bones. Perhaps it will be me who finds the formula.

A mother like this turns you into a cheesy magician pulling rabbits out of hats and scarves out of ears—but nothing works, and she isn't impressed. Remember how in the movie *Sideways* everyone is just so daunted that Miles is even *writing* a book, regardless of the fact that it never gets published? You can write a book, get it published, and even sell enough copies that your publishers are thrilled with you, but unless Oprah has you on her show to talk about it, or you make the *New York Times* best-sellers list, you are a failure. The disapproving mom has stories at the ready about how well everyone else's kid is doing. "Did you hear, Marion's daughter just bought an island with the money she made inventing an alternative fuel source from sweat, and next week she's climbing Mount Everest with five orphans strapped to her back, are you going to finish that turkey club?"

How Being an Overachiever Affects Your Life

Overachievement can add a wonderful sense of purpose to your life. It can bring rewards to you and your whole family, and it can enrich your friendships. But it can also create exhaustion! Even on days when you feel accomplished and on top of the world, you are worn out. At the end of the day you don't go to bed, you pass out. You also run a higher risk of depression, caused by self-doubt and fear of failure. When your self-worth is based on your accomplishments, you are vulnerable to the tides of fortune. Your sense of self-worth is contingent upon the approval of others and is no longer within your control. Hence, on a good day, when everything's going your way, you have high self-esteem, but on a bad day you feel like you could fall apart. In the next section I'll look at all the ways your quest for perfection could be bringing you more pain than joy . . . and what you can do about it.

Tales from the Treadmill: Jordan

To anyone outside looking in, Jordan was at the top of her game. She was a traffic reporter, like the ones you see on your local wacky morning TV shows. She was one of those folks who tell you that there's an overturned tractor-trailer blocking your favorite exit and you'll have to find a second favorite for the day. Jordan was not only on TV, she gave a radio traffic report too. And she did both at the highest level possible, as she worked in New York, which is the top, top market for any broadcaster, regardless of what they're broadcasting. In the morning you saw her cute little cherubic face on camera, letting you know that the roads were icy and parking rules were in effect today citywide. Then in the afternoon, she reported on the traffic for the drive-time show on the number-one radio station in the number-one city in America. Jordan was rumored to be dating an anchor on a national news channel, which was confirmed when she showed up on his arm to the Christmas party that year. For Jordan, it wasn't enough.

It was too easy that she got to this stage of her career by the age of twenty-five; she no longer felt challenged. The classic overachiever, Jordan needs constant stimulation and something to strive for. She became restless. She began to feel depressed regularly and to make the lives of everyone around her miserable. She was always being told she was "too" something: too belligerent; too saucy; too determined to wear hot pink on air though she had been warned repeatedly against it. Jordan was too over it!

continued on next page

... *continued from previous page*

A high-profile job can service the overachiever only when it still allows some wiggle room. When you get to the top of your game, you need to make a lateral move, and that's what Jordan did. She admits, "Everyone was shocked when I announced I was leaving at the end of my contract, because they could not imagine what else I could possibly want. They all began throwing money at me to get me to stay, but that wasn't what it was about for me. I was miserable and bored and needed more." Jordan was dealing with some delicious peer pressure. Her friends weren't traffic reporters; they were hosts of cooking shows. Jordan decided that if she were going to be on television she would rather say "three-bean salad" than "three-car pileup." Jordan went to culinary school to become a chef, and she now enjoys the pressure of wondering how well her cooking show is doing in the ratings, whether she'll get canceled or moved to a national show again, what can she do to stay current (or currant, in this case), and whether she'll sell a cookbook in the meantime. Jordan bellows, "The thrill is back, baby! The endorphins are full-flow!"

2

How Does Overachieving Affect Your Life?

Being an overachiever can have an impact
on every aspect of your life and the lives of the
people around you. The secret is to make sure
that impact is positive.

Chapter Two

The Effect on Your
Home and Family Life

The way we define "family" is so unique
to our world right here, right now.

In fact, there is no one definition anymore. Here's what I mean: According to the U.S. Census Bureau, in 2006 the number of unmarried couples living together surpassed the number of married ones, adding another new definition of family to an already long list. Your family might consist of you, your partner, and a dog; you might have the average nuclear family—a husband and a couple of kids; or maybe it's you, living alone.

And the word *home* has many different meanings for overachieving women. A crazy-busy stay-at-home mom with an endless array of events—be they social, academic, or parental—needs a more structured home, while a powerful, single executive might rarely even be at hers. Mazzy and her best girlfriend, Fiona, are the perfect illustration of how overachievers' homes can be reflections of their lives, and how contrasting and distinctive they can be.

Mazzy runs a division of Sony and her life is booked solid. She spends every single day engulfed in her artists' marketing and promotional lives. Lunch may take her across the country; dinner is eaten on her way to one of her artists' performances. There are CD signings, TV appearances, radio interviews, and tours. If she is in town long enough to go home she's trying to catch up either on sleep or on paying her bills. The last time Mazzy "entertained" was when she handed a bottle of water to the cable guy on his way out the door. She keeps meaning to unpack those last few boxes in the hall closet—she's just never home long enough. (Oh, did I mention she's lived in that house for five years?)

On the other end of the continuum is Fiona. On her résumé it would simply say that she is a mother of three who works as a proofreader, but her day planner says otherwise. As well as working and raising her children, she is helping plan her sister's wedding and helping remodel her mother's kitchen. As she paced through showrooms with her mom looking for a kitchen sink, she got the idea for her own small remodeling plan. It started with ripping up the living room; then she decided to add on another bedroom and a state-of-the-art bathroom as well. Her project has now ballooned to thrice the size.

Mazzy's home is an ignored piece of real estate that, if she just spent some time on it, could not only be a wonderful place for company—perhaps even a date—but could also have some serious resale value. Fiona's home now reflects the chaos she feels inside, the chaos that is ironically her comfort level. Maybe it works for her, but for her husband and children it's just bedlam and it's driving them crazy.

Why Home and Family Are Important

Where you live, how you live, and with whom you choose to live are reflections of what you're feeling inside. In turn, you affect your environment—and the others who live in it with you. The importance of your relationship with your home should not go underappreciated, so before we get into your relationships *at* home, let's discuss your relationship *with* your home itself—the actual housing unit where you live to keep your brown suede Manolo boots safe and warm. See if any of these examples make sense to you.

How You Live

If Your Home Is Completely Organized, It Says . . .

After a day of being torn in several directions and having to work hard to control every aspect of your delicately balanced life and schedule, the last thing you need is to come home to a disorganized desk, dishes in the kitchen sink, or a pair of shoes lying right by the doorway from three days earlier when it rained (yes, I think they're dry now!). You need your home to be clean and organized, and, like

Don't try to tackle it all in one fell swoop. Instead of telling yourself that you're going to get the entire house organized, break the job down into more manageable tasks. Start with the kitchen or something even smaller, like one drawer. Tackle each area one by one, and in a few weeks you'll find you can even get to that pile of stuff in the basement. Alleviate stress by taking small steps toward the larger goal of a clean, organized home. Don't worry, you'll get there.

Set a time. Scientists have found that the key to getting a task done is to set a time to do it. You are much more likely to get your closet organized if you say to yourself "Saturday at 2:00 p.m. I will do the closet" as opposed to "I should get around to cleaning out that closet sometime."

Be systematic. If you are a list maker and a chart-aholic, then this tip is perfect for you! Make a list or put a chart together that includes each part of the house you want to organize, and break each part down into specific tasks. In the kitchen, your tasks might be: organize the bottom drawer; rearrange the pots and pans; give the refrigerator a spring cleaning; find the expired products in the back of the pantry; and restock the shelves. As you achieve each task, check it off your list or make a note on your chart. Then reward yourself with something nice, like a bath or maybe a yoga class.

Delegate. If you have a family, then it is your right as the mom to delegate who does what. Get your husband or partner involved in bringing order to your house, and teach your kids early that cleanliness is indeed next to godliness! The kids can sort through their old toys and books for ones they don't use anymore; your husband can sort out his tools in the garage, or maybe he can tackle that dreaded bottom drawer in the kitchen. Getting everyone else involved will help you keep your sanity while teaching them all a lesson about taking responsibility and having respect for what they own.

Hire someone. No matter where you live, you can hire a closet organizer. (I mean a person who organizes closets for a living, not someone who is "in the closet" about how orderly they like things to be.) It may be worth spending the extra cash to have some peace of mind. My stepfather always tells me that you can never put a price tag on peace of mind, or on what your time may cost you. The cost of an organizing service may pale in comparison to the expense of taking a few hours away from your business. Check your local Yellow Pages for professional organizers.

Ditch your outdated wardrobe. I once heard an amazing tip for deciding what clothes to get rid of. At the change of a season—when you switch your wardrobe from winter to summer, let's say— hang all of your clothes with the hangers facing backward. Each time you wear something, when you put it back in the closet, face the hanger the right way round. At the end of the season, you should get rid of whatever is still facing backward, because you didn't wear it and that means you no longer need it. Another tip is to try not to get too sentimental about your wardrobe. Your purple chenille sweater might remind you of the night of your first kiss at a Psychedelic Furs concert, but the band parted in the early nineties, just as you and your sweater should have.

Make some cash. Once you've cleaned out your closet and organized every room in the house, what do you do with all those clothes, toys, old appliances, and little tchotchkes you don't want cluttering the house up anymore? Have a yard sale or give an online auction site like eBay a shout-out. You know the old adage: One person's trash is another's treasure. And if you earmark your profits for something you really want and know you'll use—hmm, let's say a Coach bag— everybody wins.

Set up a storage system. Everything in your house needs its own little spot to be returned to every time it gets used, so allocate specific cupboard drawers, boxes, and hooks for all your worldly possessions. For example, if your closet is besieged with shoes, stack them in pairs one on top of the other in the boxes they came in. (If you have already thrown the boxes away, go out and buy some shoe-box-sized boxes.) "But how will I know which shoes are in which box?" you say. Get a Polaroid camera, take pictures of the shoes, and tape them to the outsides of the shoe boxes. In some stores that specialize in storage solutions you can buy shoe boxes that have little windows on the front for pictures. (This tip works for organizing everything from T-shirts to hair accessories to tools.)

continued on next page

to do . . . continued from previous page

Be preemptive. Develop a "clean as you go" philosophy so that after you finally do organize everything, it doesn't turn into a frightful mess all over again. That might mean setting regular times during the week to do chores, and it definitely means making sure that everyone in the house uses the storage system you've set up. They have no excuse anymore to just shove stuff in any cupboard or, worse still, leave it lying around. Stay on top of things day by day and your house will stay clean and organized so that you can focus on the more important issues in life . . . like how many licks it really takes to get to the center of a Tootsie Roll Pop.

Make sure your problem isn't something bigger. Most people who live in a disorganized mess end up that way because they never get around to cleaning up, but some have a more serious issue called hoarding behavior. For them, hoarding can be a way to relieve anxiety. For example, a woman who is afraid of death might create an unbelievably disorganized mess as a way of staving off death. Somewhere in her brain this makes sense because she would be mortified if she died and her family found her in this horrible disarray. She thinks: "I can't die if I have cleaning to do; I'm not done yet." Hey, I didn't say it makes sense—unless it does make sense to you, in which case you may have a real issue, solvable with therapy. If you think there might be deeper issues underlying your disorganized mess of a house, it's time to talk to a professional about it.

me, you can't even think when there are dust bunnies underfoot. To you an unmade bed is a statement for all womankind that says, "Oh, heck, I don't care anymore, just come and take me away." A tidy, well-organized home brings you peace of mind and a sense of control over an otherwise chaotically busy life.

If Your Home Is a Disorganized Mess, It Says . . .

On the other hand, you may thrive on mess. But you may be un-aware of the implications. Keeping an untidy home can be a passive-aggressive way of keeping yourself out of the house and moving: If your home causes you stress, you stay away, which forces you to keep occupied. A cluttered, disorganized, poorly decorated living space doesn't lend itself to relaxation. Instead, your home is a giant version of that junk drawer in your kitchen that you swear you'll get to one day (and perhaps you do, but a week later it's back to clutter). This is bigger than just having a messy house: It's a testimony to what's truly going on inside you—a mirror for your fears of not suc-ceeding. Your closets are probably filled with things you don't need and that are taking up precious space. If you truly want to get past your mental block, this is your metaphor. Get rid of all the junk you don't need; organize your home; and embrace the success that you deserve. You worked hard for it, don't you think?

If Your Home Is Practically Empty Inside, It Says . . .

One of the most successful women I know—a classic overachiever who runs a company employing nearly seventy-five folks—lives in a lovely high-rise apartment building, the kind that makes her fellow New Yorkers envious because it has a washer and dryer right in the apartment, and a balcony large enough for a forbidden barbecue grill. With the exception of a bed, she did not have one piece of fur-niture in that place for nearly two years. She sat on her bed to eat, read, and do her toenails when she didn't have a moment to get a pedicure. She kept meaning to at least go online to find a chair, a coffee table, something other than a box to keep her television on, but the days kept slipping by. Crisis after crisis at work took priority over everything else. She took her responsibilities to her employees and their families seriously. On her one day off she would attend the wedding of the daughter of an employee before she

to do   Advice for the Empty-Room Girls

Not having "me" time is one thing, but not having—oh, I don't know, maybe a couch—says a lot about where you fit in on your own priority list. It says you feel you are not as important as everyone and everything else in your life. It's time for that to change. You're so good at being there for others—now it's time for them to be there for you. It's okay to ask for help. Ask a friend with great taste and a little time to spare if she or he can help you work out what furnishings you need and the best places to get them. You can write a list and go into a showroom that you trust and buy everything at once. Or you can buy separate pieces one by one. If you choose the latter approach, just make sure that you consistently set aside a day each month to hunt for the perfect rug, or some cute throw pillows, or whatever you have budgeted for this time around. Don't forget that looking at catalogs and Web sites at home can save you from traipsing for hours from store to store. If you purchase furniture that needs to be assembled, you might be calling on that friend again—but also check to see if the store offers an assembly service for a reasonable price. It can mean the difference between having a table to eat dinner at and a big box in the middle of the room to keep stubbing your toe on.

would go furniture shopping. She might not have had any "me" time, but she was a great boss and was dedicated to her company.

Where You Live

You Rent an Apartment

Not every overachiever is in a secure fiscal position in her life at present. We may be striving to get there—and get there we will—but some of us are still products of our overextended, underbudgeted, highly expensive lives. When you hear *overachiever* keep in mind that the word doesn't necessarily mean *rich* and *successful* in the traditional sense, as many overachieving women measure success in their own special ways. Some of us are still burdened by student loans or business loans—or maybe taxes and the prices of things are higher than we would like them to be. While we're getting on top of our finances, renting is just right.

And then there are those of us who choose to rent so we can live in a big city, where all the jobs and business contacts are. For some frantically busy women, access to services at any hour of the day or night—catching a late-night subway home from the office, dropping off their dry cleaning at midnight, squeezing in a haircut on their way home from dinner—is more important than having a chunk of the suburbs to call their own.

You Have a Nice House in a Clean Suburb

In a nice suburb you are privy to all of the upcoming overachievers

Tales from the Treadmill: Sarina

One evening on my nightly radio show I asked my overachieving listeners to call in and tell me about their experiences. Sarina called me on her cell phone while sitting in the parking lot, listening to my show and waiting to pick up her son from his karate lesson.

She told me that when her son got in the car and heard our topic, he had said to her, "Mom, you have to call in, she's talking about you!" to which she'd replied, "Oh, you think I'm an overachiever?" (So often it's only the people we live with who notice our behavior—we haven't gotten the memo yet.) As her son rolled his eyes as high in his head as humanly possible, she'd dialed the phone to call in to my show.

Sarina went on to admit that every dinner she prepares for her family is a gourmet meal. She has an interior design degree and works with a builder to construct new homes, handling all aspects of a building project: She works with an architect, oversees the building of the house, and does the interior design. Her family's own house was built thanks to Sarina's efforts, and she is now in the middle of building ten houses. Oh, and she has two teenagers.

Sarina feels that she became an overachiever out of necessity when her son was two years old and her daughter was a newborn and she suddenly became a single parent working two jobs. But the older her children got and the less they needed her, the more things she added to her to-do list.

Sarina is the self-proclaimed neighborhood taxi, she regularly hosts lunches for all the other ladies, and come December she has a

Christmas party every weekend for a different group of people. She has a walk-in safe in her house and all that's in it are Christmas decorations, from floor to ceiling. Immediately after Thanksgiving she enlists the help of her family to set up the house for the Christmas parties, but she admits she drives them crazy demanding that everything look perfect.

It's clear from Sarina's story that overachieving runs in the blood. Her fifteen-year-old daughter is even more of an overachiever than her academically: The teen gets straight As, placed in the top five in a national science competition, and since she was five years old has always had her homework done ahead of time.

"My mother was an overachiever," says Sarina. "My grandmother was one too. She grew up and lived on a farm and grew her own food, made her own clothes—she was better than all of us in that way."

in your neighborhood: the junior high and high school girls who are being groomed right now, in front of your eyes, to do everything and anything. You feel envious in some ways. You secretly think, "I wish someone started me earlier like that, then I would be *a lot* further along than I am now." And that's probably true, but keep in mind that the tailspin you're now living in is your own doing—as a youngster you didn't need the additional pressure.

The suburban environment lends itself to leading a high-powered life and having a respectable job while enjoying all the pleasures of the non-urban world. You probably couldn't play tennis if you lived in the city—it would be much more expensive. And forget about seeing friends, or your weekly community involvement—you couldn't be as effective in the city. You have more space, less traffic, and better schools for your kids. That said, you also have more square footage to clean, decorate, and make perfect for guests. More to stress out over during one of your perfectionist tirades—*Oh, why don't they make self-cleaning family rooms and self-pooper-scooping dogs?* Modern technology has abandoned you in this way, and it has you in a spin.

You Own an Artsy Townhouse in an Up-and-Coming Neighborhood

Your home shows that you understand the real estate market, and among all the other goings-on in your world you managed to learn enough about a particular neighborhood to make a sound investment. Well, why wouldn't you? You are perfection in every other aspect of your life, so it's only natural that you'd know how to buy a great place in which to live in an undervalued neighborhood. But now that you're done researching the housing market and schlepping from townhouse to townhouse to choose your home, whatever will you do with this extra free time? Will you buy a second gem to rent? Will you live in this lovely find until you can locate something better? Let's hope that this artsy neighborhood can help you embrace the bohemian within and quell your wanderlust so you have enough time to make over your fixer-upper home. Yes, that's what you'll do: Focus the time that you surely do not have on giving your new abode the TLC it needs. Do I smell a project?

Who's Home with You?

Perhaps you live with your parents or a roommate. No shame there—as a matter of fact, the number of people ages eighteen to twenty-nine who have moved back home is higher than ever before and is still on the rise, nationwide. Overachievers are finding it increasingly hard to afford to set up house on their own at these tender ages while establishing their careers, especially if they have gone on to graduate school. It's a financial thing, not a need-for-companionship thing.

My first apartment was a large studio—one room—that my two roommates and I converted into a three-bedroom apartment with the cunning use of curtains and screens. I was twenty-one and writing didn't pay much, so I bartended to pay my rent and to take classes from a writer at the big advertising agency Young & Rubicam to possibly learn how to make some money at the writing game. I had just graduated from college, yet there I was back in school, learning a trade of sorts; bartending; writing plays; and trying to make a name for myself in a town where there were hundreds like me. At the time, someone told me "Hard work will never betray you." And so I worked even harder in my cramped little place with my two roommates and one cat. It motivated me to get the heck out of there.

> One of the quintessential frustrations of the unattached overachiever is that her litany of accomplishments, achievements, awards, boards she sits on, and the recognition she receives in her field are undermined when people find out she is "alone."

Then again, you might have your whole home to yourself. Contrary to pop culture beliefs (*Sex and the City* aside), not every woman is looking to ensnare a man. What we have traditionally believed about being single and living alone has been turned on its ear, as we smash through glass ceilings at alarming rates and choose not to marry, or to marry later. One of the quintessential frustrations of the unattached overachiever is that her litany of accomplishments, achievements, awards, boards she sits on, and the recognition she receives in her field are undermined when people find out she is "alone." Well, I have news, people: Some women like it that way—*gasp!*—and choose the single life because it's uncomplicated and their lives are complex enough. We should rebel against the stigma that single equals unhappy.

Things can get a bit more complicated at home for overachievers who have started up their own family units. This can mean so many things these days: Perhaps it's you, your significant other, and your miniature schnauzer. Maybe you've got three kids; perhaps you're raising those kids single-handedly. The living environment you share can have an impact on your overachieving lifestyle, and vice versa. A busy job or one that requires travel could make your time at home even more tense—or make your heart grow fonder. It's all contingent upon how much support you get at home (and your willingness to accept it). If your home *is* your work, it's perhaps even more important to have the support of your partner and/or kids. When your job is to keep house and make sure everyone else is bathed, scrubbed, laundered, and well fed, there is no end to the tasks you could find to do—unless you set some limits.

The way in which you choose to live is as individual as you are. As an overachieving woman, it's all about finding the balance that's right for you, and for everyone else who's blessed to live in your overachieving world.

The Good

How great for your family that they know they can always rely on you. As the saying goes, if you want something done well, give it to the busiest person. If you are a mother, you show up to every soccer game and PTA meeting, and you make the best ballerina costume a child has ever worn in the history of the ballet recital. Your husband knows that you always have his back—you're a real team player. If you are single, you give good dates, cook a delicious gourmet meal, stay in relatively great shape, and carry on a compelling conversation at a cocktail party.

Your overachieving lifestyle benefits your relationships and home life because you embrace them with verve and passion, like a fashionista embraces a Catherine Malandrino sample sale. These kinds of activities suit you, and you're comforted in knowing that you derive a great sense of self-worth and accomplishment from them. After all, any investment in your life or your family members' lives leads to a big payoff—otherwise, why do it?

The Bad

The potential negative effect of your overachieving lifestyle on your home and family reads like Gene Shalit's scathing review of *Gigli*. You are overly critical of what your kids do, what the super in your building doesn't do, what your husband forgets to do, and even your dog's doo-doo. You would love to control this aspect of who you are, but time and again you hear yourself commenting when others make mistakes. Your standards are so high it seems everyone is letting you down. The people around you end up as stressed as you are, and they feel pressured to live up to your expectations . . . you know, the unrealistic ones.

The Better

When women are overly critical of their family members, it's usually driven by perfectionism, an urge for everything at home to be *just right*. Perfectionism is motivated, in part, by the desire to avoid failure. The first thing to realize is that perfection does not exist, and that it is in the process of trying and in your level of motivation that you can measure your worth. It's when you start to define your worth not by your efforts but by the things you didn't achieve—the failures—that you have a real problem. The "better" here is to set achievable goals, take stock after you've reached each goal, and be proud that you did so. No matter how small, every goal you achieve is in service of your larger goal. Even one step toward it is an accomplishment. This is a "stop and smell the roses" approach, and it's all about balance. Tabitha's story will show you what I mean.

> It's when you start to define your worth not by your efforts but by the things you didn't achieve—the failures—that you have a real problem.

Tabitha says: "I always wanted to accomplish whatever I set my sights on, and I wanted to get it done quickly, efficiently, and to always do it right." Once Tabitha had achieved one goal, she immediately moved on to the next. But by setting too many goals one after another, she stopped enjoying achieving them, and they started to cause her anxiety. She was working as a nurse while studying to become a doctor, and she had a husband in the Air Force, a new car, two children, and a big house that she maintained to perfection. She ended up taking her stress out on her husband and kids, making excessive demands and setting unrealistic expectations. She got so stressed that she started taking pills. Being a nurse and in med school, Tabitha knew the consequences, but she thought that she could handle it. She believed she was different from everyone else—she could use these pills to keep herself going and everything would be fine.

Snapshot of an Overachieving Mom

It's 7:00 Saturday morning and Nancy is making breakfast for all three children. Amber doesn't like eggs; Jack will only eat pancakes that are whole grain and organic (yes, he's already that kid); and Isabella needs a good solid meal before her softball game—it's a doubleheader. Nancy, our overachiever, is stuffing and licking 250 envelopes for an event the breast cancer organization she chairs is holding, while making each separate breakfast, lunch-to-go for Isabella, and cookies for the bake sale at Amber's school. She has already cleaned the house, walked the dog, ironed the four shirts her husband nearly burned holes in the last time he tried to "help out" with the ironing, and fact-checked a book report on Christopher Columbus—all in the time it takes a mere mortal to reach over and hit the snooze button twice. This overachieving mom does more before breakfast than most people do all day.

"In reality, it wasn't okay, and instead of helping me achieve the goals that I had set out in front of me I ended up not being able to do anything," she says. "In the end I lost everything, and the lesson I learned was about balance. But to learn that—to find balance—I lost the husband, the house, the kids, and I had to drop out of med school."

Tabitha took part in the twelve-step program Narcotics Anonymous to overcome her addiction and had to learn for the first time how to keep her overachieving ways in check. This was something she'd never learned growing up, because in her home the philosophy was always "full speed ahead." She has now been clean for three years but feels she is still learning about balance.

"Now I have to recognize when my mind is going too fast and stress is about to take over; when I begin to go from this to that to that to that and there's no time in the day to finish what I need to get done. I have to sit on my hands, take a breath and back up, accomplish the goals I can and stop myself from making any more."

Fortunately, a story as extreme as Tabitha's is rare—but we can all still learn something from what she went through. The take-home message here is: Achieve your goals step by step and work toward only goals that bring you—and the people who are important to you—joy.

The Types

Ah, so many types of families and ways of living—so many types of overachievers. Perhaps you see a little bit of yourself in one of the following?

The Micromanager is very good at driving her family nuts by organizing their lives to be as perfect as hers. This isn't just "Clean up your room" stuff. You know this is you if you micromanage everything in your children's lives, your boyfriend's apartment, any kitchen or living room that will have you, even where the cat sleeps—all to the tune of Frank Sinatra's "My Way." (And through it all, you just can't stand it if you don't know *everything* that's going on in the lives of those around you.) The Micromanager sets the standards, and then she makes sure we all live up to them.

The Whip Cracker nags and pushes her family to make sure that the house is spotless, the lawn is perfectly mowed, everyone's outfits are neater than those of the von Trapps, and they are singing in tune, to boot. Her family feels as if they are serving a prison sentence. It's a bit S and M, don't you think? If your motto is "Whips are for kids," then you have gone too far with your control of the house and are turning out neurotic little children to whom a sneeze will mean the bubonic plague and for whom *creativity* will be a dirty word . . . well, not dirty, nothing is allowed to be *dirty*.

The Do-Everything Woman is the one who is stressed out and overworked and overburdened with housework and a million other things, but won't let anyone else in the family do anything because they won't do it as well as she does. And if they do actually do something . . . "Oh my gosh, just stop, you're not doing it right. I'll do it!" Everyone else is just so inadequate, aren't they?

The "Don't You Want More?" Lady pushes her partner into being a career overachiever against his wishes. He is perfectly happy being an accountant—it's what he was when you met him—so why must he live your dreams and become a lawyer? If he hears you say one more time "Law school is only three years; the time is going to pass whether you do it or not," he'll scream. If you want a lawyer in the family, then you can add that to your own to-do list, but for heaven's sake, he's happy the way he is.

The Absentee Overachiever is so busy that she is hardly around: Her boyfriend, turtle, and family never see her. If this is you, hear this: Your boyfriend needs attention, your turtle needs more than just her food dish filled up now and again, and your family has an APB out on you. Everything around you is in danger of falling apart if you don't take a closer look at your priorities and spend some time at home.

Lives of History's Classic Overachievers: Josephine Baker

Think about what it takes to accomplish all that you do in a day. Picture what it would take to do all that while making yourself world-famous. Now imagine being a woman—an African-American woman—in the early 1900s and doing all of that. You have to have immeasurable fortitude and self-belief since there are no role models for you. To be a real pioneer you need more than drive. You need that extra something, along with incredible talent, to become an icon of perfection. This is Josephine Baker. If she isn't a role model of yours, she should be.

Josephine was born in one of the most disadvantaged parts of St. Louis, Missouri. Her father abandoned the family when she was a baby, so at sixteen months she was sent to live with her grandmother. Josephine received little formal education (she was schooled through fourth grade only) but she had a passion for dance, music, acting, and comedy. That passion was her driving force, her nourishment, and her mission. Before turning nineteen she had danced at the Folies Bergère, in the Ziegfeld Follies, and with the famed La Revue Nègre in Paris, and she never looked back to her somber upbringing. Josephine Baker became the first African-American female entertainer to gain worldwide fame in the 1920s and 1930s. And if you think three, four, or even six children are a handful, try twelve, because that's how many she and her husband adopted from around the world—a diverse family that Baker called her "Rainbow Tribe." Try cutting the crusts off twelve peanut butter sandwiches every day while working with the Red Cross and the Woman's Auxiliary Air Force, and fighting racism through the media.

Chapter Three

The Effect on Your **Friendships**

It's important to maintain strong relationships with people who truly get your overachieving nature— people who enhance your life and inspire you.

Some people believe that the things that happen to them are just dumb luck; others believe that their lives are the result of the choices they make. In psychology, this difference is explained by the theory of *locus of control.* If you have an *external locus of control,* you feel that others shape the choices you make. If you are guided by an *internal locus of control,* you feel that you control your own life and make choices primarily on your own. This is a helpful theory for understanding why you are the way you are. Do you think you gain respect from other people because you have earned it, or do you think that what you do essentially goes unappreciated? Can you control your own life, or do the forces around you—your friends, family, boss, society, etc.—control you?

"But I thought this chapter was about friendship!" I hear you say. Well, we overachievers are the queens of internal locus of control. We *are* the choices we make—including our choice of friends. Because we're overachievers, the people we surround ourselves with are pivotal: They need to either enhance our lives or inspire us in some way. True perfectionists are very good at trimming the fat; we can eschew any friendship that no longer contributes to our forward motion. We are so good at prioritizing that we can prioritize someone right out of the kingdom!

Why Friendships Are Important

So what is it about the friends we *do* hang on to? How do they influence us and why do we keep them around? Perception is key: Studies show that the way we perceive people to be is not the same as the way they perceive themselves. We choose our friends largely based on who we *think* they are rather than who they actually may be. When you think that you and a friend are *so much* alike, the truth is that you could have very little in common, because we project what we think onto how our friends think. Social status, personality, morals and values, attitudes about the world—the more we think someone is

> We choose our friends largely based on who we *think* they are rather than who they actually may be.

Tales from the Treadmill: Nikki

Nikki says that she's had overachieving friends just like her, but she's also had friends who don't do as much as she does and are content with just getting by or, as she puts it, "mediocrity."

"I don't judge them, even though that statement makes it seem like I do. I actually envy them in a way. It must be a nice, stress-free life not feeling like you always have to go and do and be," she says. Nikki finds it harder to maintain friendships with other "achievement freaks" (her loving term for perfectionists) because it gets competitive. Even though it can be a friendly competition, she always feels an underlying hostility.

Nikki and her girlfriend Karen decided to get in shape and made a pact to encourage each other to get to the gym, not their usual twice a week but daily. When Nikki called Karen to see if she had been sticking to her workout commitment, "She seemed offended that I would even suggest she didn't follow through. But look, we're all human; we miss a day or two." I asked Nikki how many days she had missed and she said, "None, of course."

Nikki recalls how, when she would tell another achievement freak about her long, arduous day, the woman would try to outdo her, as if that person's day was way more hectic and it was much harder to be her. These competitive friendships started to wear on Nikki, and she made a few changes for her own sanity. Now she surrounds herself with her second husband, her daughter, and friends she calls her "run-of-the-mill girlfriends," who are in fact her best friends. When I asked if any of them are among the achievement-freak squad, she said that none are. Her husband is not an overachiever by any means, although he has accomplished

continued on next page

. . . continued from previous page

a lot in his lifetime. His motto is "Work smarter, not harder." Nikki admits that her daughter is not an overachiever either and that it bothered her at first that her little girl chose the role of "social butterfly" over "straight-A student" at school. Nikki says, "I tell myself she is not me and that she will find her own way."

She says she loves both overachievers and non-overachievers. "And," she says, "I am aware that everyone is not perfect, however— just to let you know—I am still an overachiever. I have been the supervisor of quality control for a Japanese oil company for seven years. The job itself is a little controlling, a lot anal, but it has its place."

So has Nikki seen the light in terms of her friendships? Well, no, not exactly. Having friends who aren't overachievers, she feels the need to step in every once in a while. "My best friend is back in school getting a graduate degree at my insistence. I think education is power, and I told her so. In order to fully motivate her, I went to pick up her books for her first paper, and before you know it I had half of her report done for her. Again, I can't help the genes but I can definitely make the spirit better. I know that I am an overachiever, but there are different degrees. The people in your life teach you to let go . . . and then you actually have to do it."

like us, the more likely it is we will become friends. We say things like "We feel this way" (that's the *royal* "we") or "My friends and I support this idea." Even if each individual in your group of friends has a different opinion, to the outside world you feel that collectively you are a force to be reckoned with.

If we see a friend achieving great success, we feel that vicariously it is our success too. Of course, as overachievers we think we are busier than our friends and usually do things better than they do—but they live up to our friendship standards. Our standards for our friends are similar to those we have for ourselves: Busy people want busy friends because they "get" us and there is a margin of self-respect that we perceive goes with someone who has goals. Validation, self-affirmation—that's what it's all about. The power of the bond of friendship is not to be underestimated because over the course of a lifetime, a woman has more friends than romantic partners.

Some of us are closer to our friends than to our own families. If brown is the new black, then friends are the new family, and this is why you need to nurture your friendships. Your friends will never ask when they are getting grandchildren or why you can't be more like your brother. Mainly, they are the ones to whom you can disclose your inner feelings; you know they are receptive and responsive, and, most important, give emotional support in times of crisis. Friends are your secret weapon. Many overachieving women say that their friends are the only people who truly understand them. And if you don't have a significant other, your friends are all the more important to you.

The Good

In general, women have better-quality and closer friendships than men do. Our personalities make us better listeners, more compassionate, and very social. From an evolutionary perspective, this difference in personality is adaptive. While the men were out hunting and gathering, we were making friends with the neighbors in case we had to borrow a cup of grog or get a recipe for freshly killed pterosaur. (Even as cavewomen we had to multitask, with the in-laws dropping by the cave every two seconds.) Unlike men, we don't have to do things together to feel that we are friends—no need to bond over some baseball team (or, for the new metrosexual daddies, a Snugli). Just talking on the phone and sharing stories is enough for us. We

to do — Competition Busters

If you feel that a friend is in competition with you, it's up to you to pull yourself out of this relationship, because it's not based on anything real. As an over-achiever, your time is precious, precious, precious—no need to waste it on someone who keeps trying to "one-up" you. Sit back and think about the friendships in your life one by one and judge how important they are. You'll soon see that your real friends love you unconditionally, and vice versa. You and your real friends are happy for each other's successes, you cheer each other on, and you empathize with each other when things go wrong.

If you are the competitive friend, I'm here to tell you that this is zapping your energy, adding to your stress level, and possibly endangering your friendships. You need to devote your energies to more important matters and use your brain power for good, not evil. Think about the last time a friend achieved something great. How did you react? And when she failed at something, were you sympathetic? Remember that you need good friends who applaud your successes (and commiserate about your failures) just as much as they need you.

can do it on the way to pick up our kids from acting class, or while shopping for back-to-school clothes—heck, women call each other from bathrooms to check in on how each other's date is going.

Overachievers need this connection. We need to share secrets, and this privileged self-disclosure that we bestow on our closest friends helps keep us sane as we drift just a little bit toward crazy with each passing, overloaded day. Our friends are our break from it all, as well as the benchmark we use to gauge how we are doing, if we are doing enough, and whether we could be doing it better.

As overachievers we need validation. Friendships are the place to discuss the advantages of your overachieving lifestyle (because maybe you get nowhere talking to your mom). You're in good standing emotionally if your friends picture you as a role model, or as a coach and motivator to those of your clan who are on the brink of something wonderful and need a little push. Nurturing your friendships is another task you happily add to your list. It feels great to be needed by your friends—and maybe just as important, to know they'll be there to support you if you ever need it.

The Bad

Female friendships, as meaningful and special as they can be, come with a certain degree of difficulty. Throw perfectionism into the mix and they become even more complex.

Problems especially arise when a friendship is wrought with feelings of competition and jealousy. Competition arises when two friends want the same thing; jealousy occurs when each perceives that the other's success has in some way interfered with her own. This is especially true for women who have very specific goals that only a rare few can reach.

Alana and her best friend, Ann, have a lot in common. They met in a communications class so it's not surprising they have similar interests and goals: They both want to produce television, a highly competitive field where jobs are few. This kind of situation is not the best for fostering friendships between women, and Alana and Ann's friendship is cracking under the pressure. (When I tried to befriend someone at a radio station I worked at and it all went to hell due to the competitive atmosphere, my friend from college said to me: "You wanna know who your friends are? Your friends, that's who.") Competition begets jealousy, and both create difficulties in communication, feelings of frustration that you are not being entirely let into your friend's life, and, to a certain degree, mistrust.

One of the challenges of being an overachiever and trying to maintain healthy friendships is that we judge ourselves at an impossibly high level, and we tend to judge our friends at that same level. If they don't measure up, we're disappointed; we expected more from them. If you're driven to perfect your life, that's cool, but just be aware that it may be driving your friends bananas. Perhaps they're so easygoing they don't mind that you have expectations even St. Frances Xavier Cabrini would fail to live up to. But that doesn't quell your anxiety—in fact, it makes you wonder if it's time for new friends who aren't so laid-back. It's not, because this is *your* issue, and it's time you asked yourself whether anybody can live up to your expectations. You need to step back and judge clearly whether your friends have truly failed you or, like the rest of us, are simply flawed human beings (albeit ones who would give you the last piece of chocolate cake regardless of how PMS they are feeling that day).

One of the most interesting phenomena I have found is that many overachieving women feel that they value a friendship more than their friend does, and contribute more too. This inequality sets the groundwork for bitterness and hostility. When you barely have time to shampoo, let alone lather, rinse, and repeat, you begin to resent one-sided friendships. Realizing when a friendship has become unequal may be the first step to dropping some dead weight from your life. So now you're like Santa trying to figure out who's been naughty and who's been nice—as if you don't have enough going on! Remember, social relationships remain an important health resource as we age—but not if the basis for the relationship is vitriolic.

If you're married, did you find that when you started choosing bridesmaids you learned just who your real friends were? Did it make you realize which friendships were the true, long-lasting ones, and which were destined to fade? Yes, I thought so. When women get together they often talk about the meaning of friendship. It's certainly a running theme on my radio show: Women call from all over the country to try to make sense of why some friendships fall away, and to reevaluate those that last.

One night on the show I told a story about a friend of mine I had always considered an equal. She and I were the same degree of pretty,

Snapshot of You as the Overachieving Friend

Have your friends found that despite the fact they cannot afford a manservant, things are always magically getting done for them? If this is the case, you might be their overachieving friend. They want tickets to the theater? Done. Reservations for a girls' night out? Booked. Man troubles? Solved. Even if you're on the biggest date of your life, you'll take a call from a friend who's trying to plan the perfect romantic getaway, and you'll be able to list the top five vacation destinations for her. As the overachieving friend, you have no doubt that you can balance the phone, your friend's conundrum, and your fella, all at the same time. Everyone understands that you are always there . . . and there . . . and there . . . oh, and sometimes over there . . . .

the same degree of smart, and, I thought, the same degree of ambitious. We had been friends for nearly fifteen years. She was in the middle of moving—unfortunately, not in order to upgrade to a swanky new penthouse, but the opposite. She had been laid off and had to downsize while she pondered freelance positions and the prospect of no health insurance. In my world, I stand firm on the idea that friends are there for the boom times and for the down times, and friends shouldn't discriminate—but I did in this case (with good reason). It hit me that there was a problem with our friendship when there I was painting her apartment, not *with* her but *for* her while she unpacked and dawdled around the house. I lost myself in thought while doing her molding, and found that I was resentful rather than supportive. It didn't feel as though we were putting in an equal effort—and it wasn't like I had nothing else to do. At the time, I was shooting a new television show (which would never see the light of day, but I didn't know that until weeks later), doing radio broadcasts, and writing my first book, yet somehow I felt this overwhelming obligation to my friend. Since I was constantly on the move, what was one more thing (painting) to add to the list? My unsettled feeling was compounded when I was done and she barely thanked me. She just said, "Okay, thanks, call you tomorrow," as if I were a mere acquaintance rather than a close friend taking time out of an incredibly dense schedule to help out.

As I told the listening audience, something about this wasn't right, and I was trying to figure out what. Had I burdened myself with such a busy schedule that helping her seemed a chore? Why had this turned into such a non-altruistic experience for me? Call after call came in with sage advice. "Where were all her other friends, and if she doesn't have any, what does that tell you?" said one person. "You're a giver, she's a taker, and you have to just acknowledge that as the foundation for your alliance with her," said another.

I gave it all some thought. It occurred to me that the relationship had changed significantly and I had remained friends with her out of guilt at my own success and also out of obligation, since we had been friends for such a long time. She wasn't as ambitious as I was and maybe she never had been. She certainly didn't "get" me, and she never respected my time. Truth be told, this experience elucidated how far apart we had grown. As I shared this experience with other overachieving women, they nodded in agreement, since most of them had been down this road. Nobody wants to feel that they give and give and receive nothing in return, and you especially don't if you have a tight schedule with loads of responsibilities.

The Better

When it comes to friendship, women tend to get really involved with each other. Overachieving women get even more involved, because our friends become an extension of who we are: They have to represent! The key to having better friendships is understanding why the ones that aren't working for you aren't working. The people you choose to surround yourself with personify either what you want to be or what you have already been and are trying to reclaim. This means they either inspire you or help you resolve previous issues that are still gnawing at your soul. Ask yourself whose voice it is you hear when trouble stirs in your relationship with a good friend. It is your mother's? Your father's? Your boss's? Or the voice of some guy who didn't think much of you at a time when you were particularly vulnerable? Getting this clear in your mind can often help explain why some of your friends are indispensable

> The people you choose to surround yourself with personify either what you want to be or what you have already been and are trying to reclaim.

and others are expendable. Your goal should be to foster better friendships, because there is nothing like loyalty. It fuels us, inspires us, and, in the larger sense, helps to shape our worldview.

The Business of Friendship

Many women's social identity and business identity work so independently from each other that it's like they are two different people. If this is how you operate, then you may want to try applying what you know about running an office, a company, or a household to running your friendships. A great technique to help determine if it's time to make a change is to do a cost-benefit analysis—but instead of financial capital, we are discussing social or human capital.

As a perfectionist, Charlene could not leave anything undone, and that included her friendship with Ramona. After twenty-three years of companionship, Charlene felt that she and Ramona were heading in different directions, so she weighed the time she had already put in against the time she still had ahead of her. She set aside her emotions and looked at their relationship in terms of limitations versus assets. Ramona was particularly needy and grew more so as they approached forty. She was terrible at resolving conflict with Charlene and it seemed she was always mad at her about something, which was wearing on Charlene's last nerve. Charlene likened the situation with Ramona to what it was like trying to reason with her four-year-old. One day Charlene told Ramona that Ramona wasn't a child anymore and that Charlene had real children who needed her.

Ramona didn't talk to her for two weeks and when Charlene was relieved instead of hurt, she knew that the relationship no longer suited either one of them. She was the first to suggest a "break," and now, six years later, they have both moved on.

When a friendship is vulnerable to dissolution, it is the perfectionist who will notice it first. We're attuned to that sort of thing because being in control of our immediate environment is one of our secret weapons.

The Types

The Too-Busy-for-Friends Friend: Well, maybe she has time for one friend, but not an entire group, and nobody really close. This overachiever is in jeopardy because she has no true social network. When things go bad, who does she have to fall back on? Emotional and social support goes a long way . . . and never underestimate the value of "How does this dress look on me?" and "Can I borrow that Gucci bag for my date Saturday night?"

The Friendship-of-Convenience Friend: This is the woman who is so busy she has lost touch with the true meaning of friendship and spends time with other women only out of convenience or necessity. Does your social circle consist of the mothers of the boys in your son's little league, or the mothers of the girls in your daughter's class, even though you don't share anything real with these women? It's not so much that you share a friendship, more like a free taxi service. Your real friends are your college roommate and a girl you met on a teen tour—you know, the ones you can *really* talk to . . . when you remember to call them.

Everyone's **Best Friend:** When anyone comes to town—for example, second cousins of her sister's ex-boyfriend's colleague from work—this woman has to put them up, cook a five-course meal, hand-make rose-petal soap for the guest room, and press their clothes for them while they're asleep. It's okay; she has a nice house and likes to entertain—mostly to show off how fabulous she is. This woman is certainly put upon, but it's all her own doing. If she doesn't like how her housekeeper cleans, that's all right: She'll clean the house herself to perfection for the next round of guests, then spend the next few weeks interviewing new housekeepers. This is the woman who you think is a really good friend because she is so generous and hospitable—but then you see her treating a complete stranger exactly the same as you, and suddenly you don't feel so special anymore.

The Martyr Friend: This overachiever goes out of her way for her friends regularly. She picks them up at the airport or helps them cook for that special dinner party (even if she isn't invited). She just loves to be needed. On the outside, she seems happy to help. However, she always leaves feeling depressed that her friends can never be as good to her as she is to them, and will never be able to compete with her unbelievable energy. Her friends feel conflicted about their friendship because she always shows them up. They find themselves questioning whether her help is an altruistic move

Lives of History's Classic Overachievers:
Clare Boothe Luce

You think you're busy? Just imagine becoming a public figure in every career you pursue: playwright, journalist, editor, politician, and diplomat. Now that's busy. Clare Boothe set out to become an actor and worked with luminaries such as Mary Pickford, but she soon found herself better suited to writing—and write she did. In the 1930s she was an editor at *Vogue* and later at *Vanity Fair,* and as a playwright she is best known for her play *The Women.* For most of us that would be enough. But Clare Boothe Luce, inspired by her husband, Harry Luce, the editor-in-chief of *Time,* entered politics. As a Republican with an anti-Communist and fiscally conservative platform, she won a seat in the United States House of Representatives and was later appointed by President Dwight Eisenhower as ambassador to Italy. Her name lives on in the conservative female think tank the Clare Boothe Luce Policy Institute.

to bond further with them—or a way to show off all that she's capable of.

The Mother Hen Friend: Almost everyone has helped out a friend who lost a job, was dumped by a boyfriend, or had a death in the family. Taking on that kind of responsibility is just what friends do for each other. But this overachiever crosses the line and becomes too involved in the lives of her friends. It may be that she's a really great mother and feels she has to mother everyone in her wake, or perhaps her kids have grown up and no longer need her guidance so she has set her sights on you. When you tell her your husband is out of work, she jumps on a career Web site to find him a job (in between car pooling, her teaching job, and sitting on a whole heap of boards), because she has deemed it her mission to help you out. She will suggest that you move into a different house, and will call real estate agent after real estate agent making appointments for the two of you, and before you know it she has you packed up and choosing paint chips at Home Depot.

Chapter Four

The Effect on
Your Health

Your body is like a high-powered vehicle speeding you from one goal to the next. You need to keep it in peak condition.

No discussion of the overachieving lifestyle would be complete without looking at its impact on your health. First off, if it weren't for us overachievers, where would the health and fitness industries be? I'd bet that 95 percent of all gym memberships are purchased by people who have the ambition but not the drive to make use of them—we overachievers are the 5 percent that help the gyms look full. You just know that the home treadmill came about because some overachieving woman kept being kicked off the one at the gym after an hour. Then there's WebMD. It's for women who have no time to go to the doctor; we have to diagnose and go, go, go! I'm also sure that the salad bar was created by a perfectionist woman who needed to have control over her salad fixins from the ground up. And before overachieving women came along, the triathlon just

Tales from the Treadmill: Corinne

When it comes to our health, overachievers have an advantage over mere mortal women that psychologists have a term for: "benefit finding." Since overachievers tend to be optimists with high hopes for the future (why would we work so hard otherwise?), we tend to handle adversity better than other women. For instance, while many women diagnosed with breast cancer become depressed and anxious, overachievers tend to find personal resources such as awareness groups and chat rooms, and to see the opportunity in a downward turn in health. Illness gives us an enhanced sense of purpose, spiritual growth, closer ties to others, and a profound change in perspective and life priorities. The research supports this. What makes overachievers truly unique is the way we handle adversity. We don't say, "Oh my, I have breast cancer." We say, "I'm going to start a breast cancer organization." Corinne is an amazing example of this.

Corinne, a newlywed, quit her job with Social Services and started substitute teaching while going to school at night. After being married for only four months, she discovered she had breast cancer.

"I wasn't going to let it get me down at thirty-four years old. I had a mastectomy and chemo for six months. I still worked and went to school and I scheduled my chemo for Thursday, so on Friday I wouldn't work and would have the weekend to recuperate. This worked out fine. As soon as chemo was over, I started having reconstruction surgery.

"I took a job as a teacher assistant and traveled to several community colleges to take courses that were not available at the university. At one time, I was working while going to three different colleges, and taking five courses in order to stay on track. During that time, we bought a house, moved, and I switched to another school as a teacher assistant, while continuing to go to school." (She maintained a 3.50 GPA.) "I continued to do this for six years before finally graduating. I also decided to volunteer for the local Relay for Life team in our county, which is a fundraising organization to raise money for the American Cancer Society. Each year we set our goal higher. Well, I do, but it's always okay with my husband.

"He and I also run a private mobile deejay service on the side, which we started when we got married. I am now a teacher in my fourth year of teaching. My daughters are now twenty-three and seventeen. The oldest is married and has a son. My youngest will soon graduate and start college. I continue to volunteer for Relay for Life, which requires a lot of work, and this year I decided to complete my National Boards for teaching, which is a year-long process." (It is equivalent to undertaking a master's degree in a year.)

"As you can tell, I stay very busy. I guess it's in my nature and that will never change. I love it and wouldn't have it any other way. I feel that everything happens for a reason. I often feel that by surviving cancer, I can overcome anything. No obstacle is ever too big or too small; you just have to learn how to tackle it."

involved running. Suddenly a woman figured: "Heck, I'm out here and I have this bike, might as well cycle 20 or 100 miles too." Then: "I'm hot from running and cycling, maybe I'll swim." No doubt we eat so much of our food in the form of diet and protein bars because of overachieving women, too: We needed to maximize our energy and performance, and we wanted to do it fast. Come on people, it's not called "Slim on a Reasonable Schedule," it's called Slim-Fast!

Why Your Health Is Important

If you're an overachiever, chances are you already know why your health is of prime importance: because you need your body to be purring along at optimal performance. How else are you going to do the million and one things you have crammed into your schedule? Sneezes and sniffles and fatigue are not for you—there's no time in the day.

While most overachievers have heard the healthy-living message loud and clear, sometimes we forget the need to stop, revive, and survive. It's tempting to overlook that twinge in the lower back when you've been sitting at the computer for twelve hours straight perfecting a report, or ignore your gnawing hunger because making a deadline seems more important than mere sustenance. But don't forget: Like any high-performance machine, your body needs good fuel and regular maintenance. Look after your body now and it will carry you through many more glittering achievements.

The Good

Your overachieving lifestyle can be good for your health when it gets you to the gym, encourages you to eat well (the benefits of which extend to your family, too), and makes you go straight to the doctor to get checked out when something's wrong. You've got things to do; you cannot lie around with the flu.

> Acute stress actually helps your immune system respond better to infection. It builds up your immunity while helping you stave off boredom.

We all know that being an overachiever can be stressful. The good news is that not all stress is bad for your health. In fact, not all stress is "bad" stress. After all, why do so many people jump off bridges (I'm talking about the people with bungee cords wrapped around their ankles, not the other kind) or ride roller coasters? This is known as *acute stress* and we like it because it gives us an adrenaline rush, a fast jolt of energy. You get the same kind of buzz when the endorphins kick in after a really good workout . . . or a really good sale. Acute stress actually helps your immune system respond better to infection. It builds up your immunity while helping you stave off boredom.

In 1998 theorists Peter Slade and R. Glynn Owens identified a normal, healthy form of perfectionism, which they called simply "positive perfectionism." They claim that this type of perfectionism is both satisfying and good for you, like a big bowl of fiber. You are a positive perfectionist if this sounds like you: a woman who is well-organized and highly motivated, has impeccable standards, and is driven to meet her goals head-on. What keeps you going is the fact that each time you reach a goal, good things happen. For example, that park you saved from being built on so your kids can still play there?

Well, this effort landed your gorgeous mug on the front page of your local paper. The local news channel saw it and said, "Hey, let's start a segment called 'Take my word for it' starring you." Positive begets positive, and so you are motivated to strive even harder now.

Oh yeah, and here's one more testimony to why some stress can be good for you: A recent article in the *British Medical Journal* found that a high-stress life reduces the risk of breast cancer. How is that possible? The study found that high stress lowers estrogen production, and high levels of estrogen have been cited as a risk factor for breast cancer.

to do Seek Help if You Have an Eating Disorder

There are multiple pathways that lead to an eating disorder. For some it is a learned behavior from their mothers; for others there are links to a need for perfection; and for still others, controlling what they put in their mouth compensates for feeling out of control in other areas of their life. Since there are so many reasons, which are all incredibly individual, eating disorders can best be addressed with one-on-one therapy. To find a good therapist in your area go to the American Psychological Association's (APA) Web page at www.apa.org or phone them at 1-800-964-2000. The APA is a scientific and professional organization that represents psychology professionals in the United States, provides the psychologists' code of ethics, and helps to maintain the standards that you would want in a therapist. By the way, if you have financial concerns, many therapists work on a sliding scale.

The Bad

The flip side is that some overachievers strive for perfection out of neuroticism. If you are one of these lovely lasses, good enough is never good enough. You feel you could have run farther; your arms could be tighter; or you didn't have to have one of those cookies your friend baked especially for you. Perfectionism of this sort has been linked to eating disorders, among other things. Striving for perfection is one thing; thinking you're actually going to attain it is another.

You may find yourself blaming others for why you are this way, making statements like, "Well, my husband demands this of me," or "My friends are so competitive that if I don't [fill in the blank], I won't fit in." None of this is true (though to you it feels true). Mainly it stems from fear of failure—oh, everyone has it, some of us just deal with it better than others. The repercussions can be very serious, such as bouts of depression and crushing anxiety.

For some, eating healthy can become something else in your life to try to control. *Orthorexia* is a term coined by Dr. Steven Bratman, whose book *Health Food Junkies* tells the whole story: "The defining feature of orthorexia is obsession with eating healthy food and avoiding unhealthy food. The definition of healthy and unhealthy food varies widely depending on which dietary beliefs the patient has adopted . . . such as raw foodism, macrobiotics, non-dairy vegetarianism, Ornish-style very-low-fat diet, or food allergies."

And now for the bad stress. While acute stress may boost your immunity and give you a jolt of energy, stress of a more long-term or

Are You a Perfectionist?

Perfectionism can bring with it an interest in health, diet, and fitness that is so obsessive it's actually unhealthy. But how is perfectionism defined? York University psychology professor Dr. Gordon Flett devised the following scale based on his research on perfectionism.

Ten Top Signs Your a Perfectionist

1. You can't stop thinking about a mistake you made.
2. You are intensely competitive and can't stand doing worse than others.
3. You want to either do something "just right" or not do it at all.
4. You demand perfection from other people.
5. You won't ask for help if asking can be perceived as a flaw or weakness.
6. You will persist at a task long after other people have quit.
7. You are a fault-finder who must correct other people when they are wrong.
8. You are highly aware of other people's demands and expectations.
9. You are very self-conscious about making mistakes in front of other people.
10. You noticed the error in the title of this list.

Dr. Flett identified three types of perfectionists. Here they are, getting ready for a night out.

Self-Oriented Perfectionist: She expects sheer perfection of herself, so it takes her an hour to get dressed; she tries on at least eleven outfits and finally settles on the first one she tried on, all the while feeling deep down that it's not good enough.

Other-Oriented Perfectionist: She calls for perfection from other people and demands that her friends take an extra hour to get dressed—after all, they are representing her.

Socially Prescribed Perfectionist: She thinks others expect perfection from her, so she takes an hour to get dressed, then another hour asking you "Does this make me look fat?" and yet another hour to change again.

serious nature—like the kind you get if you work long hours every day for an impossible boss, or push yourself too hard 24/7 to be perfect—results in a cascade of stress hormones that can have a negative effect on your health. In fact, the American Institute of Stress estimates that 75 to 90 percent of all visits to primary care physicians are for stress-related problems. This is an important health issue that we all need to be aware of, because stress has been linked to high blood pressure, heart attack, stroke, diabetes, depression, and other serious conditions. Psychologists have found that stress—the bad kind, that is—also reduces the coping skills we all need to deal with life's day-to-day ups and downs. It's a vicious cycle.

People cope with stress in different ways. Here are three of the more common negative coping styles:

Surrender, which means giving in and letting everything swamp you rather than sorting out why your life is so stressful. It's like when a big-headed yellow Labrador rolls over and shows you her belly: awfully cute, but not very effective.

Avoidance, which means finding ways to escape. Some take extended vacations, sneak out to matinees during the week, or stay for one more drink even though their friends have all gone home. Other people use work as an avoidance mechanism: They're always busy but never seem to get anything accomplished.

Overcompensation, which means doing the opposite of what we really feel like doing, even if it's going to add to our sky-high stress levels. For example, paying for everyone's meals when you go out with friends, even though you can't afford it; or picking up your friend's boyfriend at the airport, even though you know she's about to break up with him.

The Better

If you're looking for effective ways to manage bad stress, here's what I recommend:

1. **Control:** You probably just rolled your eyes—like I have to tell *you*, a perfectionist, about control? But really, think about this. Your daily life is an exercise in control, but how often do you use control

to do Regain Control

Compulsive anything—drinking, eating, shopping—is about behavior. You've heard of obsessive-compulsive disorder (OCD), right? Well, obsessions are thoughts, and compulsions are behaviors; a person with OCD uses certain behaviors to quell troubling thoughts. I'm certainly not saying that you have OCD just because you wolf down a block of chocolate every time you're facing a deadline at work. I'm just trying to explain where your behaviors come from, and the simple answer is: your thoughts. So, when you're reaching for another cocktail, an Oreo, or a Louis Vuitton bag, ask yourself what thoughts preceded the behavior. The best thing you can do if you find that you are regularly over-doing anything is to keep a journal. Not like "Dear Diary, Jimmy sat next to me in English class . . ." but a behavioral diary. Each time you overdo whatever it is you're prone to overdo, record the following details in your diary (you might want to carry a small journal in your purse for this purpose):

when you're feeling stressed out? Rather than letting stress overwhelm you, try to get it under control and rein in your anxious thoughts. This principle extends to exerting control over the things you use for comfort during times of stress, such as alcohol, food, or shopping. You need to get control over them because overeating, a hangover, and credit card debt will simply increase your stress later.

2. Downtime: Too many of us overachievers don't take any "me" time. We feel guilty if we go for a massage or a walk, or if we just couch-potato for a few hours. We think surely there are better ways to use our time, surely there is something we *should* be doing. Take

- What I did (e.g., what you drank, bought, or ate):
- How I was feeling before I did this behavior:
- Who I was with:
- Where I was:
- How I felt right afterward:
- How I felt a day later about it:

A pattern will begin to emerge that will make perfect sense to you. For instance, you may see that you always had a drink after coworkers made your job harder, or you shopped when you were feeling lonely, or maybe you ate when you were bored. Sometimes it's certain people who bring out the worst in you. As soon as you can identify the thoughts, people, or environmental triggers that lead to a behavior, you're well on your way to changing that behavior.

a break, take care of yourself, reenergize. There are many people counting on you, and your well-being is pivotal in their lives too.

First, you need to find more downtime by identifying what in your life squanders the most time. What are your time wasters? Whatever they are—MySpace, talking on the phone for longer than you have to, making unnecessary lists—cut them out and use that time to do the thing that makes you feel good, that reenergizes you. This is highly individual and you might have to experiment a bit to find the best way to use your downtime. Maybe it's meditation. Or perhaps sitting still drives you mad and

> Take a break, take care of yourself, reenergize.

to do | Clock It

A great way to give yourself a reality check on how much you can schedule into your day is to mark all of your activities on a twenty-four-hour clock. Take a sheet of paper and draw a big circle on it, then divide the circle into twelve equal segments. Each segment represents two hours of your day. Label the segments with the hours, starting with midnight at the top of the clock. Next, write down on the clock everything you plan to do that day, including sleep, shower, eat, drink coffee, bathe, feed the kids, walk the dog, commute to work, attend all of the appointments that you have scheduled, and so on. When you can see your day on the clock in front of you, it will put into perspective what's realistic for you to schedule and what isn't.

the most relaxing thing in the world for you is kickboxing. Try new things until you find something that works for you.

3. Balancing Your Needs With Others' Needs: This is one of the toughest stress management challenges for busy women. There always seems to be someone whose needs are more important than your own. Perhaps you run your own business and have employees who count on you; or your husband may be sick; or you have a child with a learning disability. The key is learning how to balance it all so that you don't look after everyone else's needs to the exclusion of your own. It may mean accepting a bit of help—even if you really want to do everything yourself (to perfection, naturally).

One of my closest friends is the president of a billion-dollar company. When I asked how she balances the needs of her very demanding job with everything else in her life, she said, "My rule is that anything that doesn't make money or save money, I give to someone else to do."

You may not be the president of a company, but you can adopt a similar philosophy: What my friend was saying is that she isn't afraid to delegate. And you shouldn't be, either. Whether you work in an office, run a small business, or are a stay-at-home mom, if you look closely at all of your tasks you'll find that some do not require your individual expertise and can be handled by someone else. At work that "someone else" might be one of your colleagues. At home it might be your husband or children, or maybe you even want to think about hiring a cleaner or a nanny, if that fits in with your budget.

4. Time Management: Sometimes our lives are so tightly scheduled that if just one thing—*one thing*—goes wrong, it throws everything into chaos. Traffic, a meeting that runs late, or an unexpected emotional crisis—any of them can tip us over the edge. Can you change the traffic, the late-running meeting, or the emotional crisis? I didn't think so. What you *can* change are your own reactions to stress, your own internal thoughts; these are things you always have control over. If you find that you're *always* running late for something, you may need better time-management skills. Don't cram too many things into your schedule or make too many promises, because you'll inevitably end up disappointing someone. It's okay to say no to certain requests, move appointments around, and cancel or postpone engagements that aren't vital. Leave extra time in your schedule for traffic, emotional breakdowns, or any of the unpredictable events life can throw at you.

5. Set Priorities: One key to handling stress and anxiety is to think globally and prioritize your tasks. Like many overachievers, maybe you get caught up in the "now"—got to get this done and cross it off the list *now, now, now*—and you forget to think about the big picture. Every little detail pops into your mind—Did I remember Leslie's birthday? I have to fix those shelves. Did I schedule that meeting?—and, *boom,* your thoughts are elsewhere. The noise of the minute is only going to distract you. Cut out the minutiae and Zen out, babe!

Dealing with Family Stress

Stress has more of an impact on you if you have a propensity for depression. If that's the case, you really need to learn coping strategies to deal with stressful environments. And one of the most stressful environments can be family gatherings.

Sophie really doesn't like large family gatherings and especially hates weddings. She doesn't understand all the money that's wasted on the flowers and the food—not just flowers and food, but *the* flowers and *the* food, as in "How was *the* food?" After all, it's not as if we judge the soundness of the relationship by the quality of the meal.

do

Critical Thinking

To prioritize your tasks better, use critical thinking: Consider your goals the way you would if you were looking at them scientifically. If your head is filled with tasks all competing for your attention, take a minute, stop, breathe, and ask yourself:

- How do each of these tasks serve my goals in the long run?
- Which tasks are vital to achieving my goals?
- Which tasks can I delegate?
- Which tasks are critical at this moment?
- Which tasks can I leave till later?

Then write a list of the tasks that are essential to reaching your goals, in order from most urgent to least urgent. Whenever you find your head filled with competing tasks, refer back to the list for guidance; that way you won't get bogged down.

No matter what kind of stress or anxiety you're facing, whether it's a big holiday gathering at your in-laws' place, the huge wedding of your second cousin three times removed, or a headache caused by work, study, or any other part of your life, if you practice these techniques, you'll cope much better.

Measure your panic level. When you're in a situation that makes you feel anxious, rate your anxiety level on a scale of one to ten. (One is total calm and ten is anxiety so bad that you wouldn't be able to leave the house.) This step can be helpful on its own because often when you're forced to pause and take stock of the situation, you realize immediately that your anxiety is in the lower range and you're functioning just fine. If that's not the case, this is where Step 2 comes in.

Reality check. Once the anxiety has passed, give yourself a reality check. How much anxiety was really warranted by the situation? Give a rating on that same scale of one to ten.

In almost all situations you'll find that even if you felt about a six on the anxiety scale, the situation itself only rated, say, a one and a half. Remember this the next time you feel anxiety taking hold.

Smile pretty! This is going to sound so goofy, but trust me, it works. (You may want to do it when nobody's watching, though.) When you're feeling stressed or anxious, give a really big, happy-day smile. Your brain's limbic system—a key emotional center—answers to your muscles. If the muscles in your face are in the smiling position, the brain thinks all is well and calm. No, really, I'm not making this up. Try it.

Be your own yogi. Some people swear by meditation, even for just ten minutes a day, as a way to beat stress and anxiety. All you need to do is find a quiet place to sit, make yourself comfortable, close your eyes, and focus on your breathing. If you find your mind wandering back to your worries, try counting each breath in until you get to ten, start again from one, and keep doing that until your mind is free of stressful thoughts. Another approach is to develop your own mantra that you can say to yourself whenever you're feeling anxious. It can be anything you like, as long as it makes you feel calm and reassured. It might be "I'm going to be just fine" or "Keep the big picture in mind"—whatever works for you. Your own personal mantra can take your mind off whatever's making you anxious and get you thinking about something positive instead.

Try something new, such as one of the Eastern methods of relaxation exercise—perhaps a gentle form of yoga or tai chi, which can bring you joy and peace and a break from life's stressors. These methods make you feel less stressed right away, and regular practice can make you less likely to get stressed in the first place. Remember, Western culture is one of the few that separate mind and body; in the Eastern philosophies the two were never split.

Exercise. Exercise makes you feel better on two fronts. First, it stimulates the brain's feel-good chemicals called endorphins. And second, while you're exercising you're zoning out and not thinking about whatever was stressing you out—it gives your mind a rest.

Communicate. Talking to someone about what's going on in your life can really help you put everything in perspective. While telling someone your problems out loud, you may even begin to see that they aren't as bad as you thought and that there is a solution. The simple act of expressing how you feel can also make you feel less stressed and anxious. Talk things through with someone close to you— or if stress and anxiety begin to impact your life severely, consider speaking to a professional therapist.

Snapshot of a Fitness Fanatic Mom

Some images are embedded forever in your brain, such as the first time you saw a fabulous pair of stilettos with toe cleavage, a TV in the headrest of an SUV . . . or the jogging stroller. If you think about it, it's ridiculous: There's Mom jogging along with her baby fast asleep in a three-wheel carriage; she's multitasking her child's nap and her 5-mile run. When you see her stop at a light to wait for traffic—whip!—out comes the PDA. She'll use this time to plan a safari vacation, balance the family books, and throw an idea or two into her blog—today it will be in haiku. The light changes and—oh, what's this?—she spins around and with her cell phone snaps a quickie of her adorable sleeping child to e-mail over to Grandma that will just make her day!

What really makes family weddings anxiety-inducing for her is that one half of the family isn't talking to the other half and both halves use her as a go-between. No wonder she and Mark got married at the courthouse and invited only their parents and a few friends. Sophie's coping strategy is to look at the big picture. When she's asked to a big family event, she weighs whether failing to attend will cause more or less stress for her in the long run. If not going means less stress, she says that she can't make it. She knows that her sanity is more important in the long term, and her loved ones will have to understand.

Of course, saying "no" isn't always an option. If you must go to an event or gathering that you know is going to be an emotional disaster for you, express your feelings to someone supportive. An ally at a family event can be your saving grace, so if there's a family member you trust and who you feel is on your wavelength, then try confiding in him or her. Bringing along a friend to a stressful family gathering can be a great support to you as well, and it might even help neutralize any family tension. In any case, hang in there, count the minutes, and go to your happy place if you have to.

The Types

The Medical Marvel stays ahead of any medical mishap by eating really well, going to the gym regularly, getting her teeth cleaned at the dentist every three months, and having a pap smear and mammogram once a year, all while keeping a health chart for every child, pet, and parent to make sure they, too, have their shots and yearly checkups. A framed needlepoint sampler of the saying "An ounce of prevention . . ." hangs over her bed.

The Royal Duchess of Ersatz tries to project an air of perfection. She believes the "fake it till you make it" philosophy. Appearing to have a healthy body and a youthful, glowing complexion—even if they aren't strictly real—is more important to her than anything else. (And going to a surgeon is so much less hassle than spending hours at the gym or drinking carrot and celery juice by the gallon.) She's like an old-time Hollywood movie set: To the viewer it's a grand ballroom, but behind the scenes it's all wooden boards and cork, feebly held together by rope and spit.

The Single-Minded Fitness Fanatic is a perfectionist in only one area of her life. She is *always* at a yoga class (or Pilates, or spinning, or whatever else she's currently obsessed with). She's there all the time because she wants to be perfect at it—and maybe also because she's avoiding some other, less perfect, part of her life. Being so focused on this aspect of wellness makes her feel like everything is under control.

The Food Dictator reads every label on every grocery item, box, and food package. At dinner you can predict that she'll ask the waiter what kind of oil the chef cooks with, how fresh the fish is, from which ocean it came, and whether the tomatoes are those horrible hothouse ones or the good organic kind. She believes that consuming even the smallest amount of sugar or trans fat will be a setback to her health and exercise regime that even her personal trainer won't be able to resolve in a double session. If that's not bad enough, she makes you feel guilty for what you're eating and finds a way to make you feel self-conscious, even if you weigh only 110 pounds.

The Disembodied Overachiever: Body . . . what body? This woman has too much to achieve to be bothered by a pesky little thing like that. She thinks people get sick because they're quitters. Sure, other— weaker—folk might have to worry about regular checkups, watching how much salt they eat, controlling stress, and getting regular exercise, but not her. She believes she'll just somehow magically keep marching on.

Lives of History's Classic Overachievers:
Dr. Virginia Apgar

Since this chapter is about health, I can't think of a more appropriate overachiever than Dr. Virginia Apgar. She was the first woman to become a full professor at Columbia University's College of Physicians and Surgeons, and was the creator of a standardized testing method still used today to assess a newborn's transition to life outside the womb. If you're a mom, then the words Apgar score should mean something to you.

As a classic overachiever, Virginia had to have more talents than merely being an über-famous doctor. She was a highly sought-after violinist and cellist, but after her older brother's death from tuberculosis and another brother's battle with chronic childhood illnesses, she became not just a doctor but a surgeon, something quite unusual for a woman in 1929. Virginia didn't just graduate from Columbia University—she graduated fourth in her class, and while other women in her class fell by the wayside and left medicine, she won a surgical internship at Columbia. She specialized in anesthesiology, an area where there were few women, and soon moved into obstetrical anesthesia. She began researching the effects of drugs given to mothers during labor on their newborns. Despite initial resistance to her findings, in 1952 the Apgar score was born (pun intended), and it is still the standard today.

continued on next page

. . . continued from previous page

The Apgar Score

The word Apgar is itself an acronym for the key components of the score. The first A is for the baby's overall appearance: Is his or her color normal? P is for the pulse and heart rate. G (grimace) is how the baby's face reacts to the world—that is, facial movements and reflexes. The second A is for activity and movement—how the little arms and legs are moving. Finally, R is for respiration, the rate and effort of the newborn's breathing. Each component is given a score, the highest being a two. Babies are usually scored at one and five minutes after birth. An Apgar score of seven or higher means that the baby is fine. Anything lower doesn't necessarily mean that a baby is unhealthy or abnormal—it may simply mean that the baby needs some special immediate care.

Chapter Five

The Effect on Your
State of Mind

*Leading a busy or high-pressure life doesn't have
to negatively impact your state of mind.*

State of mind. We use the term all the time, but what do we actually
mean by it? It's the thoughts that run through our heads, the attitude
we greet the world with, our mental energy, our outlook on life (be
it sunny, gloomy, or indifferent), and whether we're calm and cen-
tered or bouncing off the walls. Even the faith or spiritual beliefs that
guide us can be considered part of our state of mind.

The negative side of an overachieving lifestyle on a woman's
state of mind is well documented in magazine articles and psychology journals. But being a perfectionist doesn't *have* to cause havoc
with your state of mind—it's like, all Manolos are shoes . . . but not
all shoes are Manolos.

Why a Good State of Mind Is Important

Why is it that some people can achieve seemingly limitless amounts in their lives while others can't, or are content not to? What separates women who, when faced with a setback, dust themselves off, try even harder, and succeed spectacularly from those who go home, eat a roll of cookie dough, get into bed, and pull the covers over their head? It all comes down to mental attitude.

Much of your state of mind has to do with what you tell yourself. The loop that plays in your head has an impact on your outlook on life, dictating how you handle it when the going gets tough. (Oh yes, it'll inevitably get tough sometime; you know it!) Are you good at being your own cheerleader, or do you need outside support? In psychology, people who rely on external forces to feel good about themselves are said to have *contingent self-worth.* Many of the overachieving women I interviewed for this book say they are the opposite. They have an innate confidence, which they recognized early in life, and they're good at keeping themselves motivated despite setbacks. They noticed at a young age that this was a quality most of their friends didn't possess.

To that end, we overachievers find it hard to relate when someone says she doesn't want more out of her life. We give her a certain look—just like the one your dog gives you when he's trying really hard to understand—that cocked-head inquisitive, "Huh? Come on, how can that be?" That expression comes naturally to many of us because we've been this way our whole lives. Striving for perfection is nothing new. We grew up with extremely ambitious goals for ourselves and have never looked back; it's in our nature, it's who we are, and it's how we have adapted to conduct our lives. It's the "adapted" part that I want to emphasize, because the difference between whether your overachieving lifestyle is a boon to your life or a hindrance boils down to the battle between adaptive and *mal*adaptive. It could go either way: Are you a good witch, or a bad witch? Do you use your powers for good, or for evil?

It's All in Your Frontal Lobe

The frontal lobes of the brain have a lot to do with goal attainment, and so are particularly relevant when we're talking about the overachiever's state of mind. Your frontal lobes are where you do all of your most important thinking, because they're responsible for your executive functioning, such as decision-making and understanding the consequences of your actions. They also form your emotional control center, which basically means that they house your personality. As a matter of fact, some people who have frontal lobe issues don't understand certain jokes, and others start to do things that are totally out of character. In one famous case, a man—a fine, upstanding dad who was an investment banker—had a car accident that caused severe frontal lobe damage, and afterward he began robbing banks. (No joke, you can look it up!) So your brain—and thus your state of mind—is pivotal in how you reach your goals . . . but I'm hoping felony isn't one of those goals!

The Good

If you're a certain kind of overachiever with a strong mental attitude, overcoming problems is just one more thing to add to your list. A tough challenge or distressing situation is an opportunity that sets you into overdrive. When you're faced with one of life's dramas—anything from bankruptcy to a serious health issue to a relationship breakup—you have the mental strength to fight back. The more challenging the threat, the stronger your response—after all, this is what you've been training for your whole life.

Most research shows that overachievers who strive for perfection have usually been that way all their lives. This means we have many years to develop strategies to make our perfectionism work for us, psychologically. Perfectionists who have adapted really well report less stress in their lives. Those of us who have learned good ways to cope with our perfectionist leanings, integrating them into the real world, are generally happier. For us, it feels *good* to strive for more.

There's something else too. In researching this book I came across many women who felt there was a certain amount of justice in overachieving. They felt that if they were dedicated to their goals, worked really hard, and were good people, then they would be rewarded by success. They believed that their personal contract with the universe would never let them down. In 1966 psychologist Melvin Lerner termed this phenomenon *belief in a just world:* the presupposition that the world is a fair, orderly place and justice will be served at every level. It's like a morality tale we tell ourselves over and over, and it's reinforced in movies and television shows, where good is rewarded and evil is punished. Overachievers tend to hold this belief in a just world more strongly than most people. We believe that hard work will never betray us and that the world is a just and fair place for those of us who live life on all cylinders. If we don't achieve what we set out to do, we think there must be a reason for it: We were too easy on ourselves, or we didn't deserve it because we didn't want it as badly as someone else.

The Bad

Okay, so life looks rosy to those perfectionists who have made positive adaptations to the real world and have good coping mechanisms. If you're not quite as good at melding your high standards with the world around you, you may have a harder time. When your natural perfectionist instincts are hampered, your state of mind is disrupted. At the least you can feel sad, upset, or stressed—at the worst, depression and anxiety can set in. Your usual overachieving state—what's normal for you—isn't normal for other women. So in the same way that you can't relate to mediocrity, others can't relate to your accelerated lifestyle. That situation is okay when everything's going right, but it can make you feel pretty darn lonely when you're up against it.

> Perfectionism can contribute to the irrational belief that if you don't reach a goal there's something inherently wrong with you—that you're just not good enough.

Perfectionism can contribute to the irrational belief that if you don't reach a goal there's something inherently wrong with you—

This advice is for all of you who have ever had that irrational belief that if you don't reach a goal there is something wrong with you.

When you were small, the way that you learned about life was by trial and error—yes, the dreaded E word, error. You made toast, it burned, and you learned to lower the setting. That process doesn't stop as you grow into adulthood; you still need to fail sometimes in order to learn.

When you do something successfully, you get positive feedback from the world (a feeling of achievement, praise from others), but when you try something and fail to achieve it, you receive negative feedback (a sinking feeling inside, criticism from others). We've been conditioned to believe that negative feedback should be avoided at all costs, when the opposite is true. It's what you do with negative feedback that's the true test of your character.

It would be arrogant to think that you have all the answers and know how to do everything perfectly. And, in fact, no one—except you—is trying to live up to that standard. Your colleagues at work don't expect you to do everything perfectly all the time;

neither do your husband, your kids, and your neighbors.

If fear of failure—or fear of failing to do everything perfectly—is crippling for you, some of the best techniques to conquer it come from the Cognitive Behavioral Therapy (CBT) folks. CBT is effective and relatively quick, taking a matter of weeks or months. It does require work from you, which I'm thinking you might enjoy, because active rather than passive therapy seems to fit better with the overachiever's nature. CBT teaches you techniques that help you challenge negative thoughts and fears you slip into without realizing; this includes fear of failure. Try to find a psychologist who practices CBT in your area, but in the meantime here's a fun scenario that you can apply to your own life that includes some proven, practical techniques.

Scenario: You have invented the Meow-Inizer, a device that translates kitty's meows into English. It's a brilliant idea but your prototype has been languishing in the garage for five years because you're afraid to try to manufacture and market it to the public in case it's a disaster and you become the laughing stock of your neighborhood. You're afraid to even try because you've seen other inventions fail and other people's attempts to start a business end in tears. You, as a perfectionist, cannot fail . . . must succeed . . . must, and if success isn't guaranteed, you won't even try. Well, that's the wrong attitude—here's what you should do:

1. Do your homework. Start researching inventors and how they got their devices on the market. Plan to meet once a week with a fellow inventor (call the lady who invented the Tweet-Inizer, perhaps) or someone who's in the pet-gadget industry. Focus on gearing your behavior toward learning more about your field.

2. Use your imagination. You obviously have a good one, because you've conjured up all of the reasons your endeavor can go wrong. Now do the opposite: Think of all the things that can go right. It's important to have a clear idea of both the worst-case and best-case scenarios before you try something new.

3. Write it all down. Every step you take, every move you make. . . . I'm sure the Police weren't singing about overachievers, but nevertheless, write down every little step you take toward your goal, every move you make toward it, all the research that you've done, and any ideas you've had. This is important because you can look back on your notes and see patterns of what worked for you and what didn't, then act accordingly in the future. (Oh, and when the Meow-Inizer is named one of the greatest inventions of the twenty-first century, the biographers will need material.)

4. Find a role model. This could be someone you know, or one of many pioneering women before you in history. The stories of great women inventors, scientists, politicians, humanitarians, stars, and business successes are laced with failures and setbacks. The important thing is that these women kept on trying—and that's the lesson you need to take from your own personal role model.

5. Bottom-line it. Take a piece of paper and write down what it is you want to achieve—in this case "Get the Meow-Inizer into pet stores." Beneath that, write "If I fail, I fear that . . ." and list every fear you have about failing to reach your goal—e.g., "I'll waste months of my life" or "I'll waste my

continued on next page

that you're just not good enough. That belief can deter you from making further attempts to do something you really want to do. This cuts off the possibility of taking risks, and for many over-achievers, no risk equals no reward. Needless to say, this can lead to frustration and unhappiness.

If you're the kind of person who sets high standards *and* demands complete order—for example, you use a complicated algorithm to work out the best placement for the throw pillows on your sofa, or you know when someone used your pencil sharpener because it's been moved a quarter-inch to the left—then the daily hassles and setbacks of life can get you down even more. There's no question that unachievable standards combined with an excessive need for order lead to a serious risk of depression.

Some overachievers have bought into the concept that there "ain't no mountain high enough." Well, I have news for you: Some mountains are too high, and they should be; nature made them that

to do *. . . continued from previous page*

savings." (Perhaps even "There will be a mass feline uprising." After all, cats do like to keep a certain mystique about them.) Take each fear in turn and analyze how serious a risk it is, what you can do to minimize the risk, and what strategies you can take the next time around if your fear comes true. You may not succeed at your first attempt but you will hit on the right strategy, and before you know it your Meow-Inizer will be in every pet shop in the country.

way. Rina, a professional writer who works for a public relations firm, learned this the hard way. She had a huge writing project to complete at work: developing a whole new marketing approach for her own firm. She is stellar at meeting deadlines, but her boss told her that she could be flexible with this one deadline since it was a very large project. But Rina couldn't bear to lose her crown of perfect employee who always beats the deadline, and instead of acknowledging the reality of the situation (that she needed an extra two weeks to complete the job) she drove herself, her boyfriend, and her mom crazy trying to meet the deadline. She neglected her mental state and health; barely slept; didn't eat properly; and didn't take breaks. She wore out her immune system as well as her mental energy. She reached the deadline, sure, but afterward spent a week in bed, exhausted and sick. She let her drive to always be the perfect overachiever hide the reality of the situation.

If your perfectionism is maladaptive, your internal script—what you tell yourself when things don't go as planned—may drag you down further. It may be that the true way you feel about yourself is pretty negative and you're a perfectionist because it's the best way you know to mask that feeling. Ask yourself whether your internal script is playing on a negative view you hold of yourself deep down. Are your thoughts just confirming all of your negative feelings? The problem here is that depression and negative thinking have a reciprocal relationship. The more you think negative thoughts about yourself, the more you cause yourself to believe them. This is how depression is maintained. You think depressive thoughts and as a result feel depressed . . . which in turn makes you think depressive thoughts. . . . . It's mentally tiring, isn't it? If this sounds like you, it's time to break the cycle and begin moving forward.

Don't Be a Drama Queen

Have you ever met someone who, no matter how bad your day went, hers was worse? Drama queens over-dramatize everything in their lives, as though they are the most important person in the world. They do unnecessary damage to their state of mind by amplifying relatively innocuous problems. A tiny problem that should have been nothing takes up their whole focus.

I have two friends who are sisters, Adrienne and Madeline. Adrienne is a fellow overachiever; she's a sports agent with a very active social life, about to publish her sixth book. Madeline came to stay with me when her relationship turned abusive; she showed up at my door with a broken arm, bruises, and burn marks the size of the business end of a cigarette. It was a terrible time for her and I tried my best to help her through it. Adrienne called, not to ask how her sister was doing, but to tell me that a package had been delivered to her house by accident, and the post office wouldn't come back and collect it to return it to its rightful owner. As she continued talking, her story gained momentum, becoming increasingly dramatic. She regaled me with the tale of how long she was put on hold by the postal service, how many people she had to speak with, how many days that poor, unwanted box had been sitting on her stoop. I didn't know what else to say other than an apathetic "Yeah, that's crazy," to which she exclaimed, "I *know!* You *can't* make this stuff up!"

Adrienne had much more important affairs to attend to—her sister, for one—yet all of her overachieving energy was being focused on the minutiae. It's a salutary lesson for everyone: It's easy to fall into the drama queen pattern, because sometimes it seems like a much cozier place to be than the real world—but if you get stuck in your own little dramas you might miss the bigger concerns that really need your attention. (On a happier note, the latest focus for Adrienne's overachievement is helping Madeline plan her wedding—to a really great guy.)

The Better

Attaining the ideal, balanced state of mind depends on your ability to forgive yourself. If you suffer a setback, resist falling into negative thinking; change the tone of what you tell yourself. Here's how it works: Let's say your life has gotten so busy and out of control that you haven't exercised for more weeks than you care to count. You've gained a few pounds, your clothes are feeling kind of tight, and that's driving your sweet perfectionist soul nuts. Forgive yourself, and recognize that this is just how things are

> Attaining the ideal, balanced state of mind depends on your ability to forgive yourself. If you suffer a setback, resist falling into negative thinking; change the tone of what you tell yourself.

right now. The inner you is healthy, fit, and looks great in a pair of low-rise jeans. When you can get back to exercising, you will . . . and you'll be in shape faster than anyone else.

I could implore you to lower your standards, but let's be realistic, I may as well ask you to join the LPGA tour (unless you're already on the LPGA tour, in which case—bad analogy). Instead, I'll say this: Your main objective should be to maintain a good working level of self-esteem. I want to be clear what I mean by *self-esteem*, since it's

to do   Focus on Your Successes

What are the five things you are most proud of that you created or achieved? They can be successes at work, in your relationships, in your family, or any other personal goals that you've accomplished. Write them here.

_____

_____

_____

_____

_____

_____

_____

Whenever you're having a low-self-esteem moment, review this list and celebrate what you've already achieved.

a term you hear all the time, so much so that it begins to not only lose its impact but also become a vague concept.

Global self-worth refers to your general satisfaction with yourself as a person on a global scale. This includes how you relate to others and how you see yourself in the grand scheme of things. It's your worldview of yourself, if you will. Your work and your relationships can shape your global sense of self-worth, so when you're feeling negative about yourself, remember that you've achieved a great deal in those areas, more than many other women. Sure, you may have suffered setbacks—that's a part of life—but the key here is to focus on your successes. This can help you get back on track.

There are three aspects of global self-worth: how you see yourself, how you think other people see you, and how other people *really* see you. The first two of these are within your control. Eleanor Roosevelt once said, "No one can make you feel inferior without your consent." Your goal is to remember that you're an incredibly powerful woman, intelligent and strong, and that nobody (nobody but you, that is) can make you feel bad about yourself. Don't sabotage yourself by eroding your own self-esteem.

If you don't want to work on your self-esteem, your other option is to lean on those people who see you as you would like to see yourself. Just rely on them to tell you how fabulous you are—oh, and while you're at it, give them your credit cards to hang on to because you may end up resorting to retail therapy, too, and in your state of mind you could end up with a drawer full of fluorescent leg warmers.

The Types

The Guilt-Ridden Perfectionist: This woman sets so many goals for herself that she never feels like she's achieved them all. As a result, she spends most of her time plagued by guilt. But she would be a slacker and have no place in this book if that were the *only* guilt she was racked with. She also feels guilty because she's so busy trying to achieve her own goals that they eclipse everything else in her life. (Why isn't her boyfriend talking to her? Oh, she forgot his birthday. Again. Why does the vet keep sending these reminder notices? Ah,

Tales from the Treadmill: Megan

Megan had a tough upbringing. She had three older brothers and one younger sister, and there were only seven years between the eldest and youngest. That would have made their house chaotic enough—but to make things harder, her mother was an alcoholic single mom. Megan became responsible at a very young age for caring for the household, cooking meals, and looking after her siblings, especially her younger sister.

"I became a perfectionist and overachiever in order to bring some semblance of order to my life. If I did not make straight A's, I was a failure. If anything I attempted did not conclude perfectly, I was a failure," she says.

Megan's family was very poor and she felt her only hope was to excel in school, earn a scholarship for college, and get away. She worked full-time all through high school and college, graduated cum laude with a degree

Fluffy's shots are way overdue.) Even if she does achieve everything she set out to do—while remembering birthdays, anniversaries, and her pets' vaccination schedules—she *still* feels guilt, either for the simple reason that her mind has been warped by exhaustion or that it just never *feels* like she's done enough.

The Nervous Nellie Overachiever: I worked for a president of a company once who was the quintessential overachiever. She climbed to the top of the company, had the perfect husband, the perfect

in accounting, and is now a CPA. She is forty-three and after years of therapy has learned to adapt her perfectionist instincts to the real world, but it hasn't been easy. She has had to learn to let some things go, such as the goal of having a perfectly clean home. Mostly, it was having children that caused her to soften some of her expectations. Her kids have made her take a more flexible approach to her career too. She gave up working in a CPA firm one year when she realized in the middle of April that she'd rarely seen her own children since January.

"When my four-year-old son asked me if we could have one of those dinners where we sit down and pass around the food, the decision to find a less time-consuming and stressful job was easy. I quit straightaway. Life is too short."

Megan now works in a job that allows her to manage her time around her children's schedules.

Lives of History's Classic Overachievers:
Mary Ainsworth, PhD

Mary Ainsworth was one of the original overachievers. In the time it takes most people to order a coffee at Starbucks, Mary went from young undergrad to doctor. She received her BA in 1935 and her master's degree a year later, and she finished her PhD in only three years. She joined the Canadian Women's Army Corps, achieving the rank of major, and then she went on to rock the world of psychology.

Her research on the mother-child bond and the theory she developed—which she named "attachment theory"—were a hugely important basis for most of what we know about moms and kids today. In 1953 Mary's husband took a position at the East African Institute for Social Research. She went to Africa with him and did her most significant work in Uganda. She is well-known for developing a procedure to measure how attached a child is to its mother; her procedure is called the "Strange Situation." When your pediatrician gives you advice about your child's personality, or any issue you may be having with your child, you can thank Mary Ainsworth for the answer.

Despite her contributions to developmental psychology and the acclaim she received, Ainsworth was regularly subjected to sex discrimination. She earned significantly less money than her male colleagues, even those she was doing a better job than. She fought hard for equal recognition, and because of her efforts and the affirmative action movement, she became one of the first female university professors and re-searchers to be paid fairly.

The Strange Situation

The Strange Situation is a twenty-minute mini-drama with eight episodes. Mother and infant are introduced to a laboratory playroom, where they are later joined by an unfamiliar woman. While the stranger plays with the baby, the mother leaves briefly and then returns. A second separation ensues, during which the baby is completely alone. Finally, the stranger and then the mother return. As expected, Ainsworth found that an infant explored the playroom and toys more vigorously in the presence of his or her mother than after a stranger entered or while the mother was absent. Later researchers found that culture has a stronger effect on attachment levels than does the baby's temperament, but it was Mary Ainsworth's work that gave those researchers a starting point.

house, and she used to compete even with me (her underling) to see who could swim the most laps. (She could.) But she was the most anxious little bunny I've ever seen. She would literally be flushed and trembling when she had to give a speech, and she was anxious about every decision she made, even at the highest level of the company. Everything always worked out perfectly, but she had no peace of mind. This woman personifies the Nervous Nellie Overachiever.

The Obsessive-Compulsive Overachiever: This woman has multiple lists in her head, on her PDA, on the desktop of her PC, and stuck on the fridge—lists, lists, and more lists. And so many rules: At home, the towels have to be folded *this* way; at work, the forms have to be filled out *that* way. Lists and rules are okay, but you can go too far, to the point where they become obsessive. Suddenly you're spending way too much time on obsessive-compulsive coping rituals instead of nice things . . . like sleep.

The Covert Ops Overachiever: This woman has to overachieve like crazy (get a perfect score on a test, cook a perfect meal, have the best wedding reception anyone has ever attended), but at the same time she's ashamed if anyone finds out how much effort it took her. Everything has to be perfect, but it has to look *effortless.* "Oh, I didn't even study for that test." (She was up all night.) "Oh, this little meal? It was simple." (It took three days to prepare.) "Oh, I organized this wedding in a month." (And two years.) But it's never much fun to live part of your life in secret, because then you have no one to share your fears with—or the work.

The In-Denial Overachiever: This woman barely sleeps because everything at home is under her command. (And yes, I mean *everything.*) She thinks that simply doing the cooking, cleaning, and laundry is for amateurs—she just rewired the entertainment room to put in a new surround-sound system and replaced the carpet in the master bedroom, and this weekend she'll re-tile the bathroom to replicate that quaint villa she stayed at in Martinique. She's the sole provider for her two teenage kids, but she also manages to fit in insane amounts of extra volunteer work at the school where she teaches. She looks anxious and depressed, and she's always complaining about her stupid doctor trying to put her on pills. Her friends and family try to tell her to meditate, take a break, or accept some help around the home, but she won't admit there's anything wrong: She's in complete denial. Problem? She doesn't have a problem . . . that would be admitting defeat!

Chapter Six

The Effect on
Your Future

*You always reach your goals. But for a successful future,
you need to make sure they're the right goals.*

As an overachiever you have boundless energy, drive, and ambition, and you're not afraid of hard work. If anyone on this good, green earth deserves to get the future they dream of, it's you. There's one other crucial element you should know about, though: the need for long-term planning. The most successful women look at the big picture. They have a list of short-term goals that guide their day-to-day life (e.g., to increase their sales this month, learn their lines for that Broadway audition, arrange all the food in the cupboard in alphabetical order), but they know that those goals are only in service of their much more important long-term ones (take over the company, become a Broadway producer, start a small business organizing other families' cupboards). They start big—say, where they want to

> The only way to make sure your accomplishments lead to where *you* want to go is to always have your long-term goals in view.

be in five or ten years' time—and then work backward. Keeping the long-term goal in mind, they structure their lives accordingly, making major changes if they have to—such as uprooting their family or changing careers. Their long-term goal is always in their sights. Always right there, just down the road.

And that's what your overachieving sights should be set on too. Without long-term goals you will still accomplish fabulous short-term goals, no doubt about that—but the only way to make sure your accomplishments lead to where *you* want to go is to always have your long-term goals in view.

Why Planning for the Future Is Important

You set goals so you know how to organize and structure your life. They give you an idea of what to do next—especially when you're unsure of what direction to take—and they also give meaning to your everyday existence. But while the daily to-do lists in your diary might help steer your course this week, it's important not to forget your long-term goals. You won't achieve them this week, this month, or probably even this year, but if you don't keep your eye on them, like a beacon in the distance, who knows where your little boat is going to end up?

Your long-term goals are your life's tasks. They are guideposts to follow when making decisions—and they also represent who you are as a person. The goals on your life's to-do list, and how you spend your time in pursuit of them, are incredibly individual. Those goals are more than just stuff you want to get done: When you've had a setback and your self-esteem is low, they help you remember who you are and where you're going. They point you toward who you want to become.

Long-term goals can be either social or individual. Perhaps your goal is to be a truly great parent, or maybe you want to make the world a better place by setting up a charitable foundation. Or perhaps your goals are not as lofty: You want to improve your tennis game or learn how to speak French. Either way, setting long-term goals and keeping them in sight is vital to achieving what you want in the future.

Here's an example. You love art. You minored in art history in college and have always been interested in sculpture. Maybe you don't have a real talent or desire to be a sculptor yourself, but you like the idea of working as a curator in a gallery or museum, or as an art historian. This requires either a master's degree or a doctorate in fine art, then an internship or apprenticeship with a gallery or museum. So, you need to get into an accredited program where you can earn an advanced degree. Your short-term goal is to do research on suitable courses and apply for them. In the meantime, you start writing art reviews for a local paper as a way of building your résumé. Another short-term goal may be to travel to see exhibits of important sculptors—those you will need to know and discuss in class and perhaps later on in the job. You have formulated a series of short-term goals in service of your broader, long-term one.

We overachievers have a different attitude toward our future goals than other women because we view our accomplishments differently. The goals we have already completed feel more like old friends who we really used to like than they do triumphs. The goals still ahead are our real ambition, the "us" we still have to become.

> Drive, focus, and a positive "I can get there" attitude make overachieving women uniquely capable of attaining their big-picture goals and creating the future of their dreams.

The Good

Most people have trouble visualizing the future. Some can imagine the person they want to be, but after a while their ambition starts to seem like a fantasy and they lose the passion to go after it. ("What was I thinking? As if I could run the company." "Me, a Broadway producer? I'll settle for community theater.") Some give up because long-term goals take a long time. It's there in the name, *long*-term, as in, "This takes a freakin' long time!"

Who better, then, to apply the necessary stick-to-it-iveness than an overachiever? Drive, focus, and a positive "I can get there" attitude make overachieving women uniquely capable of attaining their big-picture goals and creating the future of their dreams.

Here's a great example. I have a close friend who had a very prominent job: She was a disc jockey at a popular radio station in Los Angeles, which is the second-biggest radio market in the country. The number of people who heard her on a daily basis was enormous, and worth millions of dollars to advertisers. That was just her day job. Her real goal was to be a television reporter. She hoped that one day she could figure out a way to make it happen, but her goal seemed too far in the future for her to actively pursue it. As her overachiever friend I couldn't understand why she didn't seize the amazing opportunity of being on the radio in a major market and turn it into her jumping-off point into television. Any achievement-seeking woman would have capitalized on the situation and parlayed it into something really great. Instead, when my friend was let go from her radio station—as we all are at some point, because that's the nature of radio—she was left with nothing. No backup plan, no connections in television, nothing that could take her to the next level. She had to start from scratch, eventually landing another radio job in a much smaller market.

The woman who replaced her at the L.A. radio station had bigger goals in mind, and it was evident. I didn't know this woman, yet I *knew* this woman, because she was the quintessential overachiever. She wanted to be on radio and on television and to write—anything to get her name "out there." She turned her disc jockey position into something more by doing interviews with highly sought-after celebrities. Incendiary interviews. Her provocative interview technique sparked the interest of local television. It was clear to me that these developments were all calculated, thought out, and planned carefully. We were in the presence of a truly effective overachiever.

She found her way on to local television—keep in mind, local for L.A. is pretty darn good—but she didn't stop there. Less than two years after going on the air in L.A. as a local reporter, she had a national reporter's job on a major network. She was a tiger—someone with very clear ideas about who she was and what she *should* be doing, despite the fact that she wasn't half as good at her radio job as my friend had been. Nor would she ever be—she was just a classic overachiever who didn't see her radio job as her career so much as a stepping stone. When a focused overachiever sets her sights on a long-term goal, look out: Come hell or high water, she's going to accomplish it.

> There are no rules about how to choose your goals and no rules about how to reach them. As an over-achiever, what-ever you need to do, you can do.

The Freedom of the Overachiever

There are many theories about why we set the goals we set, but in my research for this book I've learned that each person's individual nature dictates what her long-term goals will be and how she'll go after them. And what a relief that is: You don't have to live up to someone else's standard; you don't have to follow in any footsteps you don't want to follow in. You can be a wife/mother/activist/politician, sure, but you can also be a single girl/waitress/pet-sitter/

yoga teacher. There are no rules. And that's another aspect of the "good" here. There are no rules about how to choose your goals and no rules about how to reach them. As an overachiever, whatever you need to do, you can do.

On my radio show I interview many famous women and ask them how they got to be where they are—the head of a modeling agency, an Oscar winner, a director. What I've found is that there is no *one* answer. Each woman has a distinctive start in life, as unique as she is. So when you find yourself in a situation in which you have to ask yourself, "Crap, how do I do this?"—make it up! Your belief in your abilities is what's important. And never forget: Pursuing goals is fun. It might be a challenge, but nothing beats the feeling of chasing and finally reaching a goal.

The Bad

What motivates the goals that you set for yourself? Are you the kind of person who likes to embrace new ideas, learn something, innovate, and enhance your life by trying something different? If you are, then you have what is known by psychologists as an *approach* motivation—that is, you are driven to approach new things, new challenges. On the other hand, some people tend to be motivated by the opposite urge: *avoidance*. When an overachiever is motivated by avoidance, it doesn't mean that she avoids setting herself goals—indeed, she may set herself many demanding goals. It means that those goals are her avoidance mechanism—a way of avoiding feelings of guilt, anxiety, failure, or even shame.

Here's an example. Sandy and Debra are both in their mid-twenties and work as legal secretaries in the same law firm. And both are studying to one day become attorneys in their own right. Sandy is fascinated by the law—her daily work as a legal secretary just spurs her on to want to know more, and to get involved more deeply. Debra always wanted to train to be a pastry chef and run her own business making beautiful wedding cakes. But her father is an attorney, as was his father, and every time she had dinner with her mom and dad she felt pangs of guilt when they talked about how much they wished she'd gone to law school. Sandy approached the task of becoming a lawyer because she was interested and motivated; Debra wanted to avoid disappointing her family.

The same principle applies to any outcome you're striving for. Do you set goals to approach a positive outcome, or do you just want to avoid a negative one? It's the difference between "I really want my business to generate more money than anyone else's in the industry" and "I just want to avoid bankruptcy." Clearly, you're in the "bad" zone when your long-term goals are motivated by an urge to avoid something (a negative emotion, a negative outcome) rather than an urge to approach and embrace something positive (a feeling of well-being, a positive result).

The Better

Some have said, mistakenly, that overachievers don't get things done because they're such perfectionists they can't complete a task—

nothing is ever good enough. But that's just not true. Overachievers are highly motivated and while they may have anxiety and stress to contend with, they *do* get everything on their list done. That's why being guided by the right list is so very important. The ideal situation is a healthy balance of daily and long-term goals that truly reflect who you

Self-regulation

The key to keeping on top of your long-term goals is *self-regulation*.

When you were a baby, you were unable to self-regulate. If you were hungry you couldn't ask for something to eat or go to the kitchen and make yourself a sandwich—you had to wait for your mom. But as you grew up, you developed what psychologists call self-regulation. Now (I hope), you don't start crying every time you're hungry: You deal with the hunger pangs until it's dinnertime.

This may sound a bit simple, but believe me, self-regulation applies to every aspect of your life. Self-regulation means that you have the power to modify your own behavior and your own actions in any situation. Here's a real-life instance where modifying your behavior and actions might affect achieving your long-term goals: It's your five-year anniversary at work and your boss hands you a gift: some flimsy mouse pad. You could utter a sarcasm-laden "Gee, thanks," storm out of the office, and start your career all over again at a different company. Or, you could regulate your behavior. You could say a polite "Gee, thanks" and accept the gift with grace, knowing that when you fill her chair—in the not-too-distant future—you will give your employees much better gifts.

If you let annoyances and setbacks get to you, you're only sabotaging your long-term goals.

want to be. You're an overachiever, so you're going to check off everything on your list—just make sure that you've planned for tomorrow as well as today and that your motivation is a positive one. If you have the following five points covered, your long-term goals are looking good.

1. Approach it. Take an "approach" attitude toward making long-term goals. Your goals should add something to your life, your experience, your knowledge, or at least your Rolodex. It's all about moving toward something positive, rather than merely avoiding something negative.

2. Learn rather than just "be." Studies show that if part of your long-term goal is to learn and not just to "be" something, you're more likely to reach that goal. If your long-term goal is just to "be rich," let's say, then you can do that any old way: Go get some unrewarding high-paying job and there you go, money. But if your goal is to learn more about the field that you love and continue to develop your skills in that field, you are likely to make money *and* be personally rewarded. You've heard the advice "Do what you love"—well, there's research to support it.

3. Be specific. The more specific your goal, the more likely it is that you'll reach it. Your path to achieving it will be clearer, too, because you'll know what information you need to find, what skills you'll need to develop, and possibly what qualifications you'll need to attain. Research has shown that the difference between those who can reach a long-term goal and those who cannot has to do with how much support they have, be it social, emotional, or informational. Do you have access to all the information you need to get to where you want to be? Is there a trap door? A secret passageway? Can everyone get there or are there specific criteria that you need to meet?

4. Set targets. By setting yourself realistic targets that gradually bring you closer to achieving your goal, you will stay motivated and focused. Setting yourself the goal of "Lose forty pounds" might feel so overwhelming you don't even try to achieve it, while "Lose eight pounds a month" sounds a lot more doable—and in only five

to do

Do What You Love

First, make a list of things that you enjoy doing that make you special and unique. They can be anything—perhaps you enjoy making clothing for your daughter's dolls and you want to turn that skill into cash. The more unique your idea, the more fun you'll have with it and the more it will feel like something special you've created. If you have a huge list, narrow it down to your top three.

Now, for each thing you love doing, write down everything you'll need to do to make it happen:

- What education or training will you need? Are courses available near you?
- What materials, tools, or equipment will you need? For

instance, perhaps you'll need to turn the garage into a workshop.

- If you plan to start your own business, how much capital will you need? Perhaps you know someone who could provide financial backing?
- If your new career involves being someone else's employee, what can you do to improve your chances of getting a job?
- What do you need to do to make sure that you can pay your bills during the transition period into your new career?

Doing this exercise will help you get focused on what it is that you love doing and see what you need to do to start your dream career.

Tales from the Treadmill: Valentina

Valentina had a very "here and now" approach to achievement. She focused exclusively on what she was doing right at that moment, because it was necessary if she was to be the best at it. She didn't spend time thinking about her long-term plans because she felt that if she took her focus away from the present she'd stumble at her current task. She gave 100 percent to each task at hand, but as soon as she was done she moved on to the next, which of course she became 100 percent involved in once again. She was a focused overachiever, but in the most restricted of ways.

Valentina excelled all through school and decided she wanted to tackle the film industry. Spots at film school were hard to get, but she was accepted and strived harder than anyone else in her year. She gave her all to her studies, volunteered on film crews outside of school, and worked as a waitress too. After film school she drove herself even harder, working seven days a week, often all through the night, until she had carved herself a niche in the competitive world of movie sound engineering. She worked with some of the best in the business and gave 100 percent of her attention to each film. Somehow she found time to squeeze in getting married and having two beautiful children.

About a decade into her career she was working just as hard as when she started. It was summer and her husband and kids had dragged her off on vacation, and while she was lying on the sand trying to relax (harder for her than it sounds), she started thinking about her career. Did she really want to go back to another film set? Did it really make her excited? Had it ever?

Lying there, she looked back over the last twenty years of her life and started to see a pattern, there under the surface. Whenever she'd had a health problem she'd always sought treatment with her acupuncturist, and had always come out feeling so much better. And the Chinese herbs she took at home were the only thing that helped her cope with the stress of her career. She thought about the calm, serene atmosphere in the acupuncture clinic. She thought about how great it must be for her acupuncturist to go to work and spend her day making people feel better. Over the years Valentina had taken short courses in subjects like Oriental massage, tai chi, and even Chinese language; and all the books on her bedside table were about Eastern philosophy and healing. It was an interest that had been there the whole time—she had just never really taken the time to think about how important it was to her.

Valentina started doing a bit more serious reading on Chinese medicine—it meant scaling back her work slightly, but she had a feeling that in a way this was a kind of work too. Gradually she came to realize that what she really wanted was to be an acupuncturist. Now she's back at school studying Chinese medicine, and loving it. She's working as hard as ever—studying to get great grades, volunteering at the clinic where she first fell in love with acupuncture, fitting in film jobs whenever she can to bring in some dollars, and being there for her husband and boys. She doesn't mind being busy, because now she is putting her energy into what she finds truly rewarding.

months' time you'll have achieved your goal. This philosophy can be applied to anything you want to achieve.

5. Manage anxiety. Give yourself a break now and then to just breathe, exercise, and take time to collect your thoughts. Even more important, try rephrasing your anxious thoughts into positive ones. You *are* your thoughts. And a pep talk from you—come on, what's better than that?

The Types

"Gone in Sixty Seconds" Overachiever: This woman is always frantically crossing goals off her list . . . and she achieves them, every single one, to perfection. Hanging out with her friends? Maybe next week. Catching a movie? Would love to, but that's two hours that could be spent more effectively. Going for a quiet drink? Too many calories—maybe a quick coffee might be nice one of these days. Ah, there'll be time for all that later—but life goes by in a blur—it's all over so fast.

The "What's a Retirement Plan?" Overachiever: This woman is so preoccupied with her career right here, right now—the next deal, the next rung on the ladder—that she's lost sight of the long-term view, the bigger picture. Forget a retirement plan—she doesn't know what the word *retirement* means. But she needs to set a little something aside . . . think of all those places on her (extensive, well-organized) list of fantasy travel destinations she'll be wanting to cross off, all the university degrees she'll want to complete, the home renovations. . . .

The "Oops, Forgot to Have Children" Overachiever: There's so much for this woman to do, so many places to be, so many goals to achieve, so many things to perfect . . . now, hold on, she was sure there was *something* she was meaning to do.

It's okay if you don't want to have kids—there's no law that says you have to—but if it's something you want to do, you can't put it off forever.

Overachiever Interrupted: This woman always has everyone else's long-term goals in sight. She's always there with a pep talk, a shoulder to cry on, sage words of advice. She gives her husband all the support he needs while he climbs the corporate tree; she does everything she can so her own staff members' careers flourish—sometimes surpassing her own. But the long-term goals she has for herself—completing that law degree, tracing her family tree, finally finishing *War and Peace*—just keep piling up.

The "Lost Touch" Overachiever: This woman is so focused on making sure what she's doing here and now is done to utmost perfection that she's out of touch with the whole circle of life. The present? She's got it sorted. Past and future are a bit blurrier. Her old friends gave up calling her ages ago because she just didn't keep in touch—she only sees the women in her book club now, anyway. Her former hobbies? They invented cardboard boxes and garages for storing her past life. And the future—she doesn't know what she'll be doing, but you can bet it won't involve the people and passions that are in her life right now.

Lives of History's Classic Overachievers:
Margaret Sanger

In 1931 the writer H. G. Wells said of Margaret Sanger: "The movement she started will grow to be, a hundred years from now, the most influential of all time." And most women would agree. Margaret Sanger advanced ideas that contributed to the modern feminist movement, and she was the first to champion women's reproductive freedom. As the sixth of eleven children, she knew something about birth control, or lack thereof: Her mother had eighteen pregnancies. But it wasn't until Sanger became a nurse and midwife in New York prior to World War I that she witnessed firsthand the relationship between poverty, uncontrolled fertility, and high rates of infant mortality. She was also privy to a number of deaths of poor mothers due to illegal and badly performed abortions.

In 1900 women's birth-control choices were limited, to say the least—mostly they were nonexistent. The Church made sure that any information about contraception was illegal and unobtainable. Sanger saw that women needed accurate information to have the power to control what happened to their own bodies. She knew that changes wouldn't happen overnight. The situation called for a long-term strategy—a crusade.

In 1914 she published a magazine called *The Woman Rebel,* and she later distributed a pamphlet called *Family Limitation,* which landed her in jail. In 1917, while serving time, the first issue of her periodical *The Birth Control Review* was published. The noise she made couldn't be ignored and public opinion was soon on her side. Sanger founded the American Birth Control League, which in 1942 became Planned

Parenthood. Later she took her crusade to the rest of the world and organized the first World Population Conference in Geneva in 1927.

Margaret Sanger taught us that real citizenship means disobeying unfair laws, which she did many times. She also made society acknowledge that women matter.

3

What Made You an Overachiever?

There are many types of overachievers, and you followed your own individual path to becoming the woman you are today. Gaining a better understanding of how you arrived here will help you to gain a better understanding of yourself.

Chapter Seven

The Role of
Personality

Your overachieving may have started right at the beginning of your life, as an essential part of the personality you were born with.

Why do some women become overachievers? What makes them stretch that little bit further than the rest of the mere mortals on the planet? There are multiple factors and I'll discuss them in this part of the book. I'll start with the most crucial factor of all, the one that underpins everything else in our lives: personality. Our personality is who we are. It affects the choices we make and the environments we put ourselves in—the careers we pursue, the way we interact with the world, the lifestyle we choose to live.

What Is Personality?

When I was in graduate school, one morning as I was getting ready for class my routine was halted by something I saw on TV: An author was being interviewed about his new business book. I was both shocked and surprised that he'd used a well-respected model of personality as the basis for his book. I was shocked not because he'd used this profound model but because he seemed to be claiming it for his own. The model I'm referring to is, some would argue, the most fundamental development in psychology in recent decades. It's what psychologists call the Big Five or the Five-Factor Model of Personality. Now, when you say "the Big Five" you have to, in the very next breath, attribute the model to Drs. Robert McCrae and Paul Costa. I was outraged that this author on the television didn't mention them. As a young student in 2000 you had to pick your battles, and on this day this was mine. I quickly found Dr. Costa's contact details at the National Institutes of Health and fired off an e-mail to him, to which he immediately replied, thanking me for my vigilance.

The psychology community didn't know very much about personality and how it develops until a few pivotal folks came around, Drs. Costa and McCrae being the most important. They gave us some significant answers to some very crucial questions: How does personality develop? Is it universal? Does it change over the course of a person's life, and if so, how drastically and in what ways? I felt justified in letting Dr. Costa know that his findings were being usurped by this charlatan. Then I paused and considered what my behavior—the fact I'd rushed to contact this very prominent scientist over this relatively mundane issue—said about me in terms of Drs. Costa and McCrae's Big Five personality traits. Was I higher in

Conscientiousness than I had thought? Or maybe it was Neuroticism? Hmmm. Let me tell you what the five are and maybe you can figure it out for yourself, and see where you fit in.

The Big Five

The five personality factors are neuroticism, extraversion, openness, agreeableness, and conscientiousness. We each exhibit all five of these personality factors, to varying degrees. Together they make up our whole personality. Here's how it all shakes out . . .

Neuroticism: If you're high in neuroticism it means that you're characteristically nervous and on the high-strung side, possibly with a bit of insecurity thrown in for good measure. Basically, you're prone to worrying. If you're low in neuroticism, you're generally more calm and relaxed—a California-laid-back kind of gal—and you tend to be much more secure and resilient. Overachieving women can sit anywhere on the spectrum of neuroticism: high, low, and all points in between.

Extraversion: Extraverts are highly social, outgoing, and gregarious. An extravert has lots of friends—generally she's the sort of person you love to invite to a party. Extraverts are also really energetic folks, and many classic overachievers are high in this trait. If you are low on the extraversion scale, you're more of a wallflower. You tend to be reserved socially and self-conscious and to have an overall inhibited and shy demeanor.

Openness refers to *openness to experience.* Those who are high in openness are open to anything new coming their way. They believe that the more experiences they have, the more well-rounded and possibly better prepared for life they are. Being high in openness means you're more original, creative, curious, and complex, while those who are low in this trait are more down-to-earth, have narrower interests, and are generally less creative. You're high in openness if you're not afraid of trying something new and are open to novelty—and I don't mean fake dog poo and joy buzzers; I mean challenges and experiences in life that are brand-new or a bit unusual. An open-to-it-all, "Sure, bring it on" attitude is the mantra of many overachievers. So, yes, being high in openness is usually a characteristic of overachievers.

Agreeableness has to do with how you interact with others, both strangers and those you know intimately. Are you good-natured, sympathetic, and forgiving? If you answered "yes," you're high in agreeableness. If you're critical of those around you, and rude to people such as waiters and service people, you're on the low end of the agreeableness scale. Not one of your better traits, but it's who you are nonetheless. Being agreeable doesn't determine whether you're an overachiever—but it might make your life easier.

Conscientiousness: This is the essence of the overachiever. If you aren't high in conscientiousness, then you're a lousy perfectionist, and I'd venture to guess that you're not an overachiever at all. People high in conscientiousness are reliable, well-organized, self-disciplined, and vigilant. At the other end of the scale, those with the lowest level of conscientiousness tend to be underachievers because they're careless, disorganized, and have trouble completing tasks successfully. Out of all five personality factors this one is most crucial: A high level of conscientiousness is inherent in the overachiever's personality.

Natural-Born Overachievers

The personality traits identified by Drs. Costa and McCrae are innate: You're born high or low—or somewhere in between—in each of the five personality traits. You owned these characteristics even before the doctor slapped you on the bottom, cut the cord, and welcomed you into the world. What I'm going to say next may come as a surprise, especially to parents: The current thinking in the world of psychology is that parenting has little or no influence on adult personality. This is why you get five kids from one family with five different personalities. Your brother might be really, really shy while you are completely outgoing. It's how you came assembled. When it comes to personality, research has shown that genetics has a bigger impact than life experience.

> The current thinking in the world of psychology is that parenting has little or no influence on adult personality.

Drs. Costa and McCrae and a host of others have studied personality for more than thirty years. They've tested thousands of people all over the world—and what they've found is that these five traits are the bomb! They hold true across the globe, from Estonia to China to America. The context might differ between cultures, but the personality traits are the same.

Most researchers tell us that these traits begin to stabilize by age

Problems with Personality

Personality traits can make us more susceptible to certain psychological problems. Depression is perhaps one of the most common psychological disorders; it affects an enormous amount of people—and overachievers are by no means exempt.

Diondra is a self-proclaimed overachiever. A mother of two, she holds double master's degrees: one in marriage and family counseling, the other in law. She graduated with honors in the top 1 percent of her class and soon accomplished her dream: to counsel foster parents and families petitioning for adoption. It's always been important to Diondra to be the best, despite the fact that her parents were easygoing about what she did with her life. They just wanted her to be happy.

Yet when Diondra began the career she'd dreamed of, she found she wasn't happy—as a matter of fact, she was the opposite. The more successful she became, the more depressed she grew. She loved her job; she loved her two children; her husband was as wonderful and supportive as could be—but still she grew more and more depressed. She'd had bouts of depression before: one time when she was in college and again, briefly, in grad school. She just assumed that once she was out of school and changed her lifestyle and career she'd be better. But she wasn't.

thirty and some traits begin to decline slowly after thirty. Some even have said that personality is not fully developed until age fifty. But *significant* changes in these traits happen only under two conditions: major life trauma and religious conversion. Environment can affect your personality—but on a small, small scale. For example, people

Studies show that women who are high in neuroticism and low in extraversion are more likely to develop depression. This is because neurotic people tend to amplify their troubles by worrying about them and those low in extraversion lack the stronger coping skills of their more outgoing sisters. Diondra's doctor did a personality assessment of Diondra and found just that: She was indeed high in neuroticism and low in extraversion. (Her conscientiousness level was off the scale, which helps explain her urge to overachieve.) Diondra decided to try therapy, combined with antidepressants, to manage her moods better. She's handling her depression the way she handles any other obstacles in her way: She reads everything there is to know about it and diligently follows her therapist's advice. Now her new project is her.

As overachievers we don't focus on ourselves as much as we should. I don't mean that we're completely selfless, because a degree of selfishness comes with the overachieving territory. I mean that we're not known for taking much downtime. This can be as a result of our personality, but it can also have a negative impact on how our personality is expressed in day-to-day life, just as it did in Diondra's case.

who are not innately high in openness who move to densely populated, culturally diverse areas tend to become more open the longer they stay there. Stress can also alter personality a bit. As far as changing your personality, that's about all of your options.

How Does It Work?

The personality you were born with may have set you up to be an overachiever and a perfectionist—but what's the mechanism that keeps the whole show rolling along? What is the fuel that feeds the fire of your overachieving personality?

Motivation

As an overachiever you are motivated in a way that most "regular" women don't understand. They call it your "drive" and they sit in awe, impressed by how long your new to-do list is at the *end* of the day. It's a marvel, and it's what makes you special. There's a great deal of argument as to what motivates overachievers, and the main debate centers on *intrinsic motivation* versus *extrinsic motivation*. Intrinsic motivation drives you to do something because you enjoy it and find it personally rewarding, such as hiking on a beautiful day, or collecting porcelain dolls. Extrinsic motivation drives you to do something to receive a reward outside of yourself, like wealth, fame, or good grades.

For many years some psychologists have argued that it's not possible to take pleasure from something you're driven to do by an extrinsic motivation. For instance, your extrinsic motivation to earn money drives you to go to work each day—and if your boss has to pay you to go, then surely it isn't something you should enjoy. To a degree, that argument's true: Most people don't like working. And research has suggested that kids intrinsically enjoy learning—until grades are thrown in and it becomes work. External rewards tend to sabotage people's intrinsic desire for and joy in certain tasks.

That's where overachievers are different. We are not only motivated by rewards such as money, success, and fame—we find striving for them pleasurable. Something that's an extrinsic motivation to a non-overachiever is to you an intrinsic motivation as well, bringing you enjoyment and personal reward. You can't tell me that checking a goal off your list doesn't give you the same kind of enjoyment other people get when they win at tennis, finish knitting a sweater, or find that rare cookie jar from 1910 to add to their collection.

As an overachiever you are motivated by grades, promotions, and success because they fulfill you; they make you feel competent and autonomous—in control of your life. This is especially true if you work in a field where much is out of your control, such as sales, entertainment, or freelance writing. Then you may be even more motivated to assert how capable you are.

Positive Reinforcement

If you've ever trained a puppy or tried to get children to behave, you know the power of positive reinforcement. What you might not realize is how much your overachieving personality may be stimulated by positive reinforcement.

Here's a familiar example of positive reinforcement. Olivia is sick of seeing her son sitting around playing video games. She really wants him to go outside to play more often. She knows that he loves hamburgers, so she decides that she will make hamburgers for dinner only on the nights that he goes out to play after school instead of coming home to play with his Xbox. Subconsciously, the boy begins to associate going out to play with coming home to his favorite food. She has reinforced his behavior with something that, to him, is a reward.

For positive reinforcement to succeed, the behavior has to have a consequence (playing in the yard leads to hamburgers for dinner), and as a result of that consequence the behavior has to be more likely to occur (Olivia's son likes hamburgers, so he goes out to play in the yard more often).

Now let's take you, an overachiever. What kind of positive reinforcement influences you? This will vary from individual to individual, but for argument's sake let's say the greatest reward for you is achievement in your career. A fact-finding committee is set up at your work to look into new areas the business might expand into. You've got a high openness level so you volunteer to be on the committee. In fact, you're an extravert and you become the chairperson of it. Even though no one asked you to, you work nights and weekends compiling all the research into a written report for the president of the company, making sure that there are no mistakes in it—you are, after all, off the top of the scale when it comes to conscientiousness. And several months later, when a new department is set up based on the recommendations in the committee's report . . . yes, you know, your name is on the manager's office door. Voilà, positive reinforcement.

Those around you have validated your innate desire for perfectionism in your own life. When someone "gets" you—when he or she sees what you're made of and is willing to support your goals—that person is reinforcing your behavior. And when your behavior is rewarded, you want to do it again. It's not unlike being addicted to a drug—but in this case the drug is your own success.

The Power of Change

When I began my research in 2000 at Columbia University, I met Professor Carol Dweck. She conducts research in the area of intelligence, and she has found that people who believe their intelligence is innate—that is, that they were born with a certain, predetermined level of intelligence—are more likely to feel helpless when they fail at a goal they've set in life. On the other hand, when people who believe that intelligence is changeable meet with failure, they don't despair, because they feel that if they work hard enough, they can achieve anything.

The lesson for all of us is that belief in our ability to change is a powerful force. Those who believe they can change are less likely to give up the fight . . . and more likely to win the prize. Without a strong belief in your ability to change and control your life, you're like a feather in the wind, prone to failure, social influences, and possibly depression if you fail to reach your goal the first time you try.

Even something as simple as throwing the perfect dinner party can give you a rush of positive reinforcement. For your last soiree, you found out ahead of time who is allergic to what, which types of seafood or mushroom everyone will or won't eat, and you cooked everyone's favorite foods and crafted the perfect night. (And I stress the word *perfect*—the food, the ambience, the wine, the music, the glittering conversation—ah, it was one of your finer moments.) The next day your friends were still raving about the delicious meal. Little did they realize they were giving you great big injections of sweet, sweet positive reinforcement. You can't wait to do it again, even though it was a Herculean task and you were up all night getting the red wine stain out of the carpet and the raspberry coulis off the dog's fur.

> When other women meet with criticism or resistance, they let it impede their progress toward a goal, but when the overachiever hears the word *no,* she goes into overdrive.

"No" Means "Try Harder"

Of course, everyone—regardless of his or her personality—is driven to some degree to want recognition from peers and family and a certain status in the community. I stress the word *degree.* Overachievers keep raising the bar higher with each passing achievement. And, unlike most people, we rarely succumb to self-doubt. If we suffer a setback we just work harder, especially if we think that we might not have a natural ability for the task at hand. When other women meet with criticism or resistance, they let it impede their progress toward a goal, but when the overachiever hears the word *no,* she goes into overdrive.

Lara was new at her company and it was up to her to put together a team for a new viral marketing campaign. (An example of a good viral marketing campaign is anything that ends up on YouTube, gets a huge buzz about it, and spreads like a virus even before it hits mainstream media.) Lara wanted a woman named Sharon on her team. Sharon had been named one of the top women in marketing by the American Marketing Association. Lara's boss made it clear that Lara wasn't on par with a Sharon. Basically, he said, "You haven't got a chance"—with an implied "You're not worthy." Lara went to work. First she introduced herself to Sharon. As soon as they started talking they realized they had a lot in common, knew some of the same people, had even gone to the same camp as children. This conversation led to Sharon asking Lara to lunch. At that lunch she revealed to Lara that she was bored with traditional marketing. By the end of the month, Sharon was on Lara's team. It takes a very unique personality to hear "No" as "Try harder."

Criticism and resistance from others dogs us all, but as an overachiever it will simply spur you on to put in extra effort—even though other aspects of your life may have to be pushed aside. Sometimes it can be your friends that fall by the wayside. Sometimes it can be your own personal grooming. (Note: Roots are only a statement if you are Madonna—the rest of us need to get to our colorist regularly.) Often it's your family's needs that get overlooked temporarily, and you hope that they will understand.

In order to quell self-doubt—that little voice in your head that says "They're right, you can't do it"—you make it all about the outcome. A successful outcome becomes your motivation, and reaching it is really enjoyable for you. It proves that you are as capable and amazing as you had suspected all along.

You're in Control

> There are many other factors that shape your behavior and the choices you make in life. You do have a free will; you are not an automaton powerless to modify your innate personality traits.

Okay, if even your parents couldn't affect how your personality developed, then you must be completely at the mercy of your genes, right? You're like a machine programmed to behave in a certain way and there's nothing you can do about it? Well, not quite, because personality is only one piece of the puzzle. It would be nice to be able to blame your disagreeable gene for your Krakatoa impersonation when the waiter brought you a whole-wheat bread roll though you specifically asked for sourdough, or your extravert gene for the fact you had a few too many drinks and did that little dance on the table at your last office Christmas party. As with most things in life, it isn't that simple. There are many other factors that shape your behavior and the choices you make in life. You do have a free will; you are not an automaton powerless to modify your innate personality traits.

For instance, a woman who is a born overachiever but is shy and dreads public speaking can, with practice, be as good an orator as the next person. An overachiever who happens to also be a chronic worrier can learn techniques to chill out and get control of her raging neuroses so she doesn't drive herself and everyone else around her mad. A perfectionist with horrifically low agreeableness (think *The Devil Wears Prada*'s Miranda Priestly) can develop skills to deal more humanely with people who don't live up to her exacting standards.

Perfectionist behavior may have been kicked off by the personality you were born with, but you are still in control. And while personality is inborn, how we acquire our values, our goals, and our expectations of life, others, and ourselves can be shaped by how we were socialized. That's what we're going to look at in the next chapter.

Chapter Eight

The Role of
Upbringing

*You came into this world with your own unique personality—
but you were also shaped by childhood experiences that
influenced your attitude toward achievement.*

My friend Claire has gotten used to the fact that her mother will
never be a cookie-baking mom who's proud of everything Claire
does just because it's *her daughter* doing it. When Claire landed a
highly sought-after job in public relations, her mother's first response was, "What can you get me tickets for?" When Claire and a
friend published a small book in paperback, her mother said, "Let me
know if it makes the bestseller list so I can tell my friends about it."
When Claire successfully established a charity with one of her
celebrity clients to help foster children, her mother said, "Why can't
he pay you? He can afford it. Why would you work for free?"

No matter what Claire achieves, her mother is never impressed.
Claire is just about to start law school and has her fingers crossed

that it may be the tipping point, the one thing that will make her mother say, "I'm proud of you."

Claire is a prime example of how a woman's upbringing can turn her into an overachiever. Claire keeps piling things on her résumé, trying to get that elusive "Good job, I'm proud of you" from her mom.

The Disapproving Parent

You were born with a specific personality, that's true, but so were each of your parents. Were their personalities a good match for yours? Did they encourage you to be who you want to be, or did they clash with you? If their personalities were different from yours, did they adapt their parenting styles to suit your individual needs? (And those of your brothers and sisters too?) Psychologists call this idea *goodness of fit*. Was the parenting you received a *good fit* for you?

In Claire's case, her mother's parenting style was not a good fit at all, and it's why she and her mother have always had a tumultuous relationship. This didn't start when she was an adult; it's been going on all of her life. Her mother didn't attend her tennis matches, or spelling bees, or any of the other hundred extracurricular activities Claire did as a child. She did expect Claire to win the spelling bees and tennis tournaments, though, and to get good grades—she just didn't consider it praiseworthy when Claire did. Even today, Claire's mother is so focused on herself that she feels Claire should accomplish great things for her benefit, to make her look good. And all the wonderful things Claire has achieved in her life haven't done the trick; they haven't given her mother the stellar achievement she wants to brag to her friends about.

This description of Claire's mother is likely to strike a chord with many overachieving women. Time and again, this kind of story comes up: a daughter constantly seeking her mother's praise, and willing to add anything and everything to her to-do list in the hope of one day receiving it.

> Claire is still feeling the effects of the bad fit between her personality and her mother's, long into adulthood.

This description may also strike a chord with those who know about the personality disorder called *narcissism*, a recognized mental condition. I'm not suggesting that all disapproving mothers are suffering from this problem, but many of them do exhibit signs of narcissism. A narcissistic woman focuses solely on herself, has a sense of grandiosity, and finds it hard to relate to other people's experiences. The narcissistic mother sees everything her daughter does as a reflection on her—it's all about her.

Claire keeps adding accomplishments to her list, but despite each addition to her growing résumé, she never feels triumphant. Instead, she ponders what to do next that might have more of an impact on her mother. Interestingly, Claire's brother, Rudy, was never as bothered by his mother's disapproving nature. He had always had a different personality than Claire—he was less motivated by the urge to please his parents. But Claire is still feeling the effects of the bad fit between her personality and her mother's, long into adulthood.

Tales from the Treadmill: Marissa

Marissa is one of the rare overachieving women who mention their father as a cause for their drive for perfection. Marissa's father has a fixed idea of what kind of a person she is, based on her rebellious adolescent days. And no matter how much growing up she has done since then, he can't see her any other way.

Marissa admits she was a terrible teenager. She was rude and disrespectful and became a runaway. She never got pregnant (before marriage), or arrested, and she didn't try alcohol or drugs, but, in her words, she acted like "a bitch" toward her parents.

As an adult, she wanted them to be proud of her. First she started a family with a wonderful, hard-working, quintessential southern man. Except for the tattoos, he was the dream son-in-law. (He remains the love of her life, and her husband today.) Still, though, her father continually reminded her of her teenage years. Her guilt caused her to add more and more to her résumé to show him that she wasn't that person anymore.

Marissa earned a Bachelor of Arts degree in French education, with a minor in Spanish. She got a teaching job at a wonderful school and started an after-school program for latchkey kids so they wouldn't have to go home to an empty house every afternoon. On the side she began making jewelry. Marissa and her husband bought their own home, a gorgeous Victorian house that she was proud to show off to her father. Still her father reminded her of her horrid teenage years. Marissa says, "He walked into our new house for the first time and said, 'I can't believe a kid who started out like you, ended up like this. We thought you'd be in jail at this age.'"

Then Marissa enrolled in a master's degree program. She was the Awards Chair for her state's Foreign Language Association; a master's degree student at Georgetown University; a French teacher at a private and very prestigious high school in Washington, D.C.; the mother of three; wife of one; cat owner; candidate for a gold belt at her karate dojo; and slowly becoming insane! Her father reminds her daily of what a screw-up she was as an adolescent. "I have done everything I can think of to make him proud of me, but I can't," she says. "I have been to hell and back . . . and it's not like my life is so easy: My son has ADHD and multiple learning disabilities, my oldest daughter has self-esteem issues, my husband has just been diagnosed with bipolar disorder, but I'm trying desperately not to fall apart. All I really want is to be forgiven for the things I have done wrong. My father will never be able to do that."

(The good news is that since I interviewed Marissa, her husband is on medication, she managed to get A's in her classes in grad school, and both of her daughters were on the honor roll at their school.)

I've talked a bit about mothers and their overachieving daughters, but not so much about the influence dads have. Indeed, growing up *without* a father (or with minimal fathering) can tend to make a girl become an overachiever. A budding overachiever in some cases "becomes" the father she needs, internalizing masculine traits beneficial to success, such as hard work, a stubborn attitude toward the word *no*, determination, and competitiveness. She sees the world the way a man would: without barriers or a ceiling on achievement. Thus an overachiever is made.

While fathers play a role in influencing our behavior, as women we find ourselves returning time and again to our relationships with our mothers when we consider what made us overachievers. When I interviewed women for this book, they seldom mentioned their fathers. If they felt that anyone caused them to become overachievers and perfectionists, it was almost always their mothers.

Heidi is a case in point. She was at her most driven in high school, where she was utterly obsessed with her grades. "I always did well but somehow that made it worse: I was always worrying about slipping even a tiny bit," she says. "It was as though my whole life would just fall apart." She was alway the best student in her English class, and the night before her final English exam she slept only about an hour—not because she was studying but because she was panicking about whether she'd perform perfectly. She did, as it turns out. But when she ranked second in Modern History she was just appalled that she had slipped from first place, out of a class of forty-two. As for Biology, coming in sixth . . . well, she may as well have failed. Heidi recalls, "I had a raging anxiety disorder about it all, and ended up being prescribed Valium. Looking back, it's just totally absurd."

Heidi was pathologically driven to achieve, and she feels that the main reason was that nothing she did made her mother give her any praise. She felt like a cat bringing in fresh kills to proudly display to its owner . . . without any effect. When she received her high school results and got the highest grade it was possible to achieve, her mother said,

"Oh, that's nice, now can you pass me those scissors?" Other kids from school were being given cars. Heidi says, "I wish I was making this up!"

As she grew up she continued to try to impress her mother, but to little effect. She worked full-time (inevitably doing overtime) in a good job while completing her master's degree. She didn't get much of a reaction. At night she studied—and excelled at—Mandarin. Still not much reaction. At one stage she was doing seven-day weeks for most of the year, fitting in a fairly senior job in health care management, a bachelor's degree in health sciences, and co-writing a book. Heidi didn't have time for anything else. When friends called to see how she was, she'd find herself feeling resentful that it was taking up fifteen minutes that she could be using to memorize a list of symptoms. If they suggested going out for dinner, she found herself thinking, "Sitting around for hours at dinner, chatting, on a Saturday night? Did they not know me?! I am way too busy for all of that inconsequential banter; I had more important things to attend to."

When the book that Heidi had taken ages to co-author was published, she proudly sent her mother a copy. She heard nothing back for a long time. Her mother did eventually read it, many months later, but appeared to be little impressed. (On the other hand, complete strangers were impressed and very supportive.)

As Heidi recounted her story I noticed that she never mentioned her father. (Her parents have been happily married for almost fifty years.) When I asked her why, she told me: "I mean, he has never been particularly effusive with praise either, yet I cut him all the slack in the world. Whereas when it comes to my mother I still, even to this day, would like a reaction."

Heidi is not alone. Many perfectionists and overachievers are fueled by disapproving mothers. We're hoping that maybe this one last accomplishment will finally make Mom stand up and take notice. We want her to realize that we matter and that what we do matters—to someone, even a stranger—and shouldn't that be enough for a little bit of praise? No? Okay, well, we'll keep trying then. . . .

Parenting Style

Another important factor to consider is your parents' overall parenting style. This includes their attitude toward discipline, their approach

to do **Break the Cycle**

If you find that you are constantly adding things to your résumé in a vain attempt to get your mother's approval, stop and ask yourself the following questions. Your answers will help to clarify the path you need to take.

- Will adding yet another thing to my to-do list in order to please my mother drain me or energize me?
- If I take my mother out of the equation for a minute and really think about it, do I want to do it?
- Will doing this task actually change my relationship with my mother?
- What is my time worth to me?
- How much time am I spending meeting my mother's needs and how much meeting my own?
- Which aspects of my life and achievements are important to me?
- Which aspects of my life and achievements are driven by guilt or even fear?

to teaching you how to find your way in the world, the way they communicated with you when you were a child, and how much warmth and affection they showed you. These factors also have a big influence on whether or not you become an overachiever. Researchers have studied the way parents relate to their children and have identified four categories of parenting styles:

Authoritative Parenting: This is a combination of warmth and control, a balanced style in which parents are involved in their child's academic and social lives. Parents relate to their child in a loving and affectionate way, but do give strict guidance when necessary. They set clear guidelines for what they expect from their child, yet they are not completely controlling.

Authoritarian Parenting: Parents with this style are highly controlling and demanding, and they lack real warmth and interest in their child's life. These are the "Do as I say, not as I do" and "Children should be seen and not heard" parents. They restrict their child's activities, social and otherwise. While it seems antiquated, this style is still pervasive. The overall message children get is: Your parents don't trust you.

Permissive Parenting: Permissive parents are warm and undemanding. They have little control over their child and place few restrictions on their child's activities. (This is fine if the activity is taking an art class after school—not so fine if it's making art by drawing all over Grandma's wall with crayon.)

Uninvolved or Neglectful Parenting: This describes a situation in which parents are indifferent about their child's life. They don't show affection, are not interested in watching their child's activities, and don't provide discipline. They don't just forget to show up for little Sally's play at school—when she tears up a neighbor's lawn for fun, there are no consequences because they are nowhere to be found. Some of these parents lack parenting skills. Others could very well be depressed; in those cases this type of parenting is a symptom of their depression.

If You Had Authoritative Parents . . .

You're a fortunate woman if your parents had an authoritative parenting style—warmth and acceptance balanced with stricter guidance and discipline when called for. This seems to be the best type of parenting. In studies it has been linked to more positive developmental outcomes, such as academic achievement, more positive feelings toward oneself, and lower levels of impulsive behavior (which helps avoid risky behavior).

If Your Parents Were Authoritarian . . .

Of all the parenting approaches, the authoritarian style is the most likely to turn a child into an overachiever. Many authoritarian parents feel that failing to do well in school or not being achievement-oriented is unacceptable behavior in a child. And unacceptable behavior needs to be punished. If your parents felt this way, as a child you may have focused on trying to avoid failure and hence their wrath. You may have developed failure-avoidant behaviors such as studying extra hard and focusing on academic goals rather than on social endeavors. The same principle applies to any other aspect of your life that your authoritarian parents felt you should strive and excel in: gym, softball, cheerleading, playing the piano, and so on. And this pattern that was set up in childhood can be carried into adulthood.

Another way that authoritarian parents tend to create over-achievers is that they demand obedience from their children, and this teaches their children the value of structure and of organizational skills. This is how someone who is not a natural born over-achiever becomes one. Even if the "Spare the rod, spoil the child" parenting philosophy—high on limits and low on warmth and love—doesn't appeal to you, it can create fertile ground for a girl to think more about goals and less about boys. (Even if she sees being successful as just a way to get out of the house!)

If Your Parents Were Permissive . . .

Permissive parents set few standards for their children to follow and try not to control them too much. They tend to indulge their children rather than force them into acceptable behaviors. These parents don't demand age-appropriate behavior from their children when it's warranted, and worse, they don't demand achievement. If their child is self-motivated, fantastic—if not, they may end up with the opposite of an overachiever.

> At its worst, permissive parenting can turn a little girl with an innately overachieving nature into an overachieving woman who stresses out when things go wrong, because she didn't develop the skills to deal with life's downturns.

It's unlikely a child could be changed into an overachiever by a permissive parent—but what happens when a child with a natural overachieving personality receives this kind of parenting? When permissive parenting is taken too far, you can get a child who has a great sense of entitlement rather than a great sense of self-esteem. Feeling good about yourself is very different from feeling as if the world owes you. This sense of entitlement can work against an overachiever because it makes it harder to get along with others and accept that you must earn your dues like everyone else.

This parenting style fits best with a child who's sensible enough not to take advantage of the situation and end up with an overblown sense of entitlement, but instead to make the most of every opportunity provided by his or her permissive parents. You want to try out for the swim team? Go for it! You want to do a summer abroad? Great idea! You want to work two full-time jobs while you're in school so you can buy a car? We support you!

At its worst, permissive parenting can turn a little girl with an innately overachieving nature into an overachieving woman who

do   Deal with Disappointment

If you never learned the skills to cope with disappointment as a child, when something goes wrong or you fail to achieve something the first time around it can feel like the end of the world. You need to learn to put disappointment into perspective. Here are some points to remember next time disappointment strikes.

Try to see the bigger picture.
Things didn't go your way this time but that doesn't mean things will never go your way.

Life has ups and downs. Look around at your friends: Does everything always go right for them, or do they sometimes have to face disappointments? It's a fact of life that we all have good days and bad. The important thing to remember when you're down is that you will be up again.

Learn to give yourself a break.
Set achievable goals so you don't consistently set yourself up for disappointment.

Turn to the ones you love. Despite the ups and downs, the achievements and disappointments, what remains constant throughout is that your friends and loved ones will still cherish and respect you.

Learn a sense of duty to the community. It has been shown that the number-one way to develop a sense of empathy for others (as well as high self-esteem) is to do volunteer work and other activities that contribute to society. In fact, doing something for your community has been shown to alleviate all sorts of problems, from boredom to binge drinking and beyond. It gives you a sense of belonging and an amazing sense of well-being, and it's life affirming. Choose an issue in your community that is dear to your heart. It could be homelessness, animal welfare, the need for better lighting in the park your kids shoot hoops at—anything you have an interest in that will make your community a better place. I know you're probably already very busy, but even a couple of hours once a month will make all the difference to your community (and to you). You'll find that the most successful women all do some kind of community work.

stresses out when things go wrong, because she didn't develop the skills to deal with life's downturns. Since she grew up without limitations and was told constantly that the world is her oyster, she can't figure out how to deal with disappointment. Nobody prepared her for that. Also, permissive parents tend to overlook moral and spiritual development in their children, leaving them with less empathy and sense of duty to the community at large. Sometimes an awareness of your place in the wider world can really benefit you as you navigate your way through life's to-do list.

Giftedness

So far we've seen how the type of parenting we received has a strong influence on whether we become overachievers. There is another crucial event during a girl's upbringing that we also need to consider: whether she was identified during childhood as "gifted" or, on the flip side, found herself in the ranks of the average and ordinary.

The Gifted Girl

Simply being gifted does not mean a girl is destined to be an overachiever. For proof, look no further than all the gifted girls with loads of potential who are lying on couches doing absolutely nothing across this great land of ours. Whether a gifted girl grows up to become an overachiever depends on not just her aptitude but a range of other factors: her personality, her schooling, her parents' attitudes toward education, and the kind of expectations that were placed on her or that she placed on herself.

> Whether a gifted girl grows up to become an overachiever depends on not just her aptitude but a range of other factors.

A gifted girl's education can in fact turn her into the very opposite of an overachiever. If her parents weren't educated and didn't value education then she, too, may not. Growing up in a neighborhood with overcrowded classrooms and teachers with bad attitudes also doesn't encourage a gifted girl to be all that she can be. Many gifted girls I knew felt like they were smarter than their teachers and so had little motivation to learn and achieve. While there are programs in public schools for children with learning disorders and other impairments, for many gifted girls there is nothing. In some neighborhoods, a gifted girl's goal might not be achievement so much as growing up and getting the hell out of there. The exception to this rule is the gifted girl with a strong overachiever personality. Girls who came hardwired for overachievement make their own way in the world, even if they have few opportunities. They find a way to get what they need.

Maribelle is an example of how a girl's personality, giftedness, and the right upbringing can come together to produce a positive outcome: a healthy attitude toward achievement. Maribelle was an intellectually gifted child, with the personality to match. She spent her early years in a trailer park in an area of northern Florida where the school system had a horrible reputation. Luckily, her mother recognized Maribelle's giftedness early and began to move the trailer around the area, making sure that the trailer was always in a good school district. This contributed to Maribelle's future potential because she became interested in school and motivated to learn. Studies have shown that gifted children will, on their own, seek out environments where they can explore their own interests, and that is just what Maribelle did: She found a summer camp program for gifted kids. That opportunity, coupled with her education in a better school district, put Maribelle in a much better position to achieve. She is now a pediatrician who also does pediatric research and is on a team that was just awarded a very prestigious grant to study perinatal cardiology.

A factor that causes some gifted girls to become overachievers is the pressure that comes with the tag "gifted." It can be pressure from parents and teachers who expect a gifted girl to perform to a very high standard. Or it can come from within: A gifted girl may feel driven to an incredible degree to live up to her gift, and to avoid failure. More is expected of a gifted girl, regardless of where those expectations come from, and this can lead to a powerful desire to achieve. The urge to achieve can be a wonderful and positive force in a girl's life, but it's important to keep stress under control, particularly at this tender age. Parents and educators can play a role in helping gifted girls navigate the expectations that have been placed upon them and those they have placed upon themselves.

The Mediocre Girl

Now on to the mediocre girls, of which I may indeed have been one. Here we're talking about C students who have no particular talent and have to work hard for years to excel—as opposed to those who excelled right out of the womb. It takes some of us mediocre girls ten years to become an "overnight success," unlike our gifted sisters whose innate abilities for science, music, drawing, and so on, were recognized right away.

The world is made up of people who aren't looking to be champions, but instead are happy to lead an ordinary life. Not everyone wants to stand out from the crowd, or do a lot of work to develop a talent they weren't naturally blessed with. Women like this realize they may be average to some but that they are special to others—and that is just fine.

To others, *mediocrity* is an insult, a curse word—and it is not an option. Such a woman will work as much as she has to in order to distinguish herself. She has to do more, learn more, and train more than other women to get where she wants to go: She is the quintessential overachiever. For her, this started way back in grade school, when it became clear that her name would never be called out first in class when the teacher was handing out test results ranked in order of achievement; or that no one would fight to have her on their softball team; or that she would

> She knows deep in her overachieving soul that these people just didn't realize her greatness—and she's going to do everything in her power to show them they were wrong.

be a camel in the Christmas play *again*. She knows deep in her over-achieving soul that these people just didn't realize her greatness—and she's going to do everything in her power to show them they were wrong.

Let me tell you about an actress I interviewed on this topic—let's call her Devin. In reality she's a working actress on a television show that you definitely would have heard of. Before we began the interview, she was clear with me that when people call her a workaholic

to do | Set Achievable Goals

I am all for kicking against mediocrity, but the goals you set yourself do need to be achievable. If you follow these pointers, you'll be using all your precious overachieving energy on the right goals for you.

Get a grip on reality. At thirty you may not have a shot at becoming the world's next supermodel, regardless of how strong your urge to fight mediocrity is or how long your legs are. Similarly, *American Idol* may not be the place for you if your singing is only good in the shower. Face facts, there are some goals that you're just never going to achieve. You need to be realistic about your capabilities and your limitations.

Think like an editor. An editor hones in on the key message of a newspaper story, book, or movie and edits out the rest. Take that same perspective when making major decisions about your goals: Edit and keep editing, and keep refining. As you grow and change, your abilities change, and so should your goals and ambitions.

Count 1, 2, 3. When choosing a career path to follow, look at whether you can answer "yes" to all three of the following questions:

1. Can I make money doing this?
2. Will I enjoy doing this?
3. Do I have a talent for this?

she takes offense. "It is affiliated with 'aholic,' the idea that something is bad for you, like alcoholic or whatever it is you are addicted to. If I'm living my passions and it just takes time to do them, then who cares? Why should I get labeled?"

In high school Devin was in a band, tutored younger kids for money in subjects that she was comfortable with, and waitressed. Devin's high school didn't have cheerleaders so she fought to get a squad started—and obviously had to become head cheerleader. She always knew she wanted to act and was very involved with the drama club and, no surprise, was the lead in every play. "Oh and I also ran track," she says. Her grades, however, were average and, as she puts it, her looks were "nothing special." Devin says she knew she wasn't as talented or beautiful as some other girls but always felt that shouldn't stop her from living not just her dreams, but her wildest dreams.

Devin says that she works hard because it brings purpose and meaning to her life. And Devin doesn't just work . . . she *works*. Aside from acting in a television show she is also a playwright and just started a theater company where she pairs writers and actors to perform original pieces on stage. "The way I see it, everyone is in therapy, or reading self-help books to find what I have already found: my purpose and my meaning, and it means the world to me. I feel great every day and love what I do and worked hard to get to this point to say this." During my interview with Devin, her phone rang: It was her agent calling to tell her that she'd just been nominated for an Emmy. Let's hear it for mediocrity!

You're in Control

Many of us overachievers carry the pain of disapproving, uninterested, demanding, or authoritarian parenting into our adult lives. Others are more fortunate and had parents who understood our innate overachieving personalities and provided just the right amount of encouragement and guidance necessary to produce well-balanced, well-equipped young women ready to take on the world, relatively free of baggage.

> You didn't have control over the way your parents raised you, or the expectations that were placed upon you by parents and teachers, but you *do* have control over how you live your life now, as an adult.

Wherever you fall on that broad spectrum, there is no denying that the patterns that were set up early in your life by your parents are strong and enduring. But while the patterns of childhood are strong, there is always a chance for change. You didn't have control over the way your parents raised you, or the expectations that were placed upon you by parents and teachers, but you *do* have control over how you live your life now, as an adult.

Just stop and think for a minute how different your opportunities are from those of your mother at your age. Then think of the options that were open for your grandmother. The world has changed an extraordinary amount for women. You are not fated to keep repeating the pattern set by your mother, and by her mother before her. We are living in a generation where all the old family rules have weakened and the realm of acceptable behaviors, especially for women, has expanded.

If, as an adult, you have come to realize that the "oughts" and "shoulds" your parents imposed upon you (how you ought to feel, what you should do with your life) don't match who you are, then you don't need to be constrained by those old family patterns any longer. There is no moral authority you need to answer to, other than your own spiritual and moral beliefs.

do Challenge the "Oughts" and "Shoulds"

If you feel there's a disconnect between the way your parents raised you to believe life should be lived and how you truly believe life should be lived, it's time to work out what's right for you. You're entitled to live as you wish, and the sooner you do that, the happier you'll be.

Listen to yourself. Does your inner monologue match with how you're living your life, or do you sometimes find yourself questioning your choices at a deep level?

Just be. Your best authentic moments can happen when you're simply having fun and relaxing your mind, so try to regularly take time out to relax and get in touch with your feelings.

Value yourself. Make a list of the five values that are most important to you in life—not what your family values, but what you value. (For example, one person's list might be: spirituality, integrity, independence, empathy, openness.)

Know what you need. Now make a list of your top five needs in life (for example, financial freedom, being my own boss, a loving home life, freedom to express myself, an environment where I can keep learning).

Live it. Use all that you've learned about your true beliefs regarding how life should be lived. Gradually put these beliefs into practice. If this means departing from your family's viewpoint, be honest and open with them about why you're making some changes in your life. Reassure them that you will always love and respect them—you just need to be yourself.

to do Adaptive Parenting

Wouldn't it be great if parenting advice was doled out like the movie times and locations you can call up from your phone? For a well-adjusted child, press one. For a child who is not living up to her potential, press two. For a child who is so out of hand you're not sure what to do, press three. All other callers, stay on the line and a psychologist will be with you shortly. [Air Supply tune on Muzak: " . . . lost in love and I don't know much . . ."] Since that isn't an option, I'll tell you that studies on parenting all support the idea that parents with the moderate parenting style known as the authoritative style are the best at balancing their own demands and emotional responses with their child's innate temperament. This parenting style is the most effective for nearly every child because it respects the child's autonomy, which lets her or him flourish as a unique individual, and provides guidance and discipline in bite-size pieces. Here are some tips:

- Remain firm but let your child know that he or she can have an opinion too.
- Don't compare your child to other children and especially not to his or her siblings.
- Be a keen observer of your child's temperament and personality, and parent that child, not the idealized child you have in your mind.
- Stimulate your child's thinking by encouraging her or him to help with decision-making and generating solutions to problems as they arise.
- Be firm on rules and help your child understand that there are consequences to his or her actions, both good and bad.
- Be consistent. Children need a predictable, stable environment, and lack of one can lead to serious long-term effects on their sense of security later on.

Our mothers lived at a turning point in history: In greater numbers than ever before they began to enter the workforce, get divorced, and raise their children single-handedly. This had an impact on what we perceived women were capable of. Our generation has taken it a step further, gaining more civil rights and economic rights. The concept of the man "bringing home the bacon" is long gone—mostly because it's so high in nitrates and fat, but also because we can buy our own. (In fact a January 2007 *New York Times* analysis of census data determined that more American women are now living without a husband than with one. In 2005, 51 percent of women reported living without a spouse, up from 35 percent in 1950.)

In so many ways the choices open to you and the options for how you live your life are broader than in previous generations. However, one thing has remained constant, and probably will in future generations: Most women's lives continue to center on raising children, no matter how busy we are with other goals. If we choose to have kids, we're usually in charge of organizing their day care, rides to softball games, the packing of lunches, the making of costumes—the overall primary care of our kids. We will keep control in this domain for one main reason: No matter how career-focused women are, we will never prioritize work over family to the same degree that men do. Perhaps this is because we actually carry the child, or because a sense of duty to future generations is built into us by evolution.

Whatever the reason, this is another really important way in which *you* are in control. If you choose to have children, you are in the same position as your mother was: The way you raise your children will influence their attitude toward achievement in adult life. You could be the mother who adapts her parenting style to her daughter's unique personality and individual needs—helping her to develop a positive attitude about achievement; helping her to become the woman she wants to be.

Chapter Nine

The Influence of
Self-Esteem

*Whether you have strong self-esteem or poor self-esteem,
how you view yourself can have an impact on how
you view achievement.*

Women have been known to rank themselves among their peers. The phrase *keeping up with the Joneses* had to come from somewhere, right? Some woman—let's call her Mrs. Smith—who lived next door to a family named Jones saw Mrs. Jones carving out quite an exquisite topiary, in the shape of an angel, for her front garden. Mrs. Smith's yard paled in comparison and suddenly she felt the need to compete with Mrs. Jones by cultivating the suburb's ultimate front lawn. Maybe Mr. Jones was a hottie who drove a sports car and looked fabulous in it, as did Mrs. Jones, and this made Mrs. Smith even more desperate to one-up Mrs. Jones. This ranking of importance was only Mrs. Smith's perception. Maybe in reality Mrs. Jones was miserable because her hottie of a husband was—ahem—a little too "friendly" with his secretary. Or maybe Mrs. Jones was tormented by an aching sense of failure because her landscape gardening business went bust, and this was her way of finding redemption: by creating the world's most perfect topiary angel. When you perceive that others' lives are marvelous while yours is average, you make this perception based on how you feel about yourself, your *self-esteem*.

Simply put, self-esteem is how you feel about who you are deep down inside. It consists of a number of aspects, including: social comparison (*How do I rank among others?*); how good you feel on a particular day (*I got a raise today, therefore I'm smart and competent*); your identity, including your social identity (*I belong to a cool group of friends and we do amazing things with our lives*); and, finally, your overall sense of self-worth. Your sense of self-worth is based on how capable you feel and how valuable you feel in the world.

Both strong self-esteem and, at the other end of the spectrum, poor self-esteem can be powerful causes of overachievement and perfectionism. Think of it like the sunny side and the shady side of the street: Though they're a bit different, they lead in the same direction.

> Both strong self-esteem and, at the other end of the spectrum, poor self-esteem can be powerful causes of over-achievement and perfectionism. Think of it like the sunny side and the shady side of the street: Though they're a bit different, they lead in the same direction.

Strong Self-Esteem and the Overachiever

The legacy of the feminist wave of the sixties and seventies is that we have a vast realm of possibilities when it comes to deciding what we want to do with our lives. Careers that were once open only to men (or to a handful of extraordinary pioneering women) are now ours for the taking. Raising a family well is no longer the only goal for us to aspire to, as it probably was for your grandmother and perhaps even your mother. If you want to focus all your energy on raising a family, that's a totally valid choice—the difference is that you now have a choice. And being a mom doesn't mean you have to give up career aspirations. You can juggle as many things as you want: No one's going to stop you.

Women have grabbed this opportunity with both hands. *Overachieving* women have grabbed it with their hands, their feet, and even their little pinkie toes. I can be a lawyer? I can be a businesswoman? I can be a great mom? I can be a blogger with an adoring cyber audience? Well, maybe I'll be *all* of those things (and maybe I'll do everything in my power to be the best at them too).

I believe that the social changes that have allowed women greater freedom have given us all a huge boost in self-esteem. I think it shows in the terminology that women increasingly use to describe themselves. More of us describe ourselves with words once considered masculine, such as *individual, assertive, outspoken,* and *independent.* The way in which you describe yourself says a lot about how you feel about yourself, and your level of self-esteem. And if you feel confident and capable of doing anything and everything, you're more likely to do just that. Feeling confident in your abilities gives you the drive to tackle more new goals—to do more, to be more. Feelings of self-worth can predict the level of career status you think you're capable of achieving.

Self-Esteem and the Overachieving Stay-at-Home Mom

Remember when the idea of housework was as anti-feminist as corsets and housecoats and the term *housewife* was more of an insult than a career choice? Well, if you have chosen to be a stay-at-home mom, I have some very interesting—and very good—news for you. Traditionally, being a homemaker was seen exclusively as a female role, while a man's role was to be the provider. Now women can go out and earn, just like their male partners, so when a woman stays home to raise children and look after the house, it is because she made a choice to do that. And for an overachieving stay-at-home mom, this choice shows a higher level of self-esteem than ever before.

First off, self-esteem is higher when women succeed at roles that are psychologically essential to them, such as raising children—what could be more essential than that? If the job is important to you and you do it well, then your self-esteem will be raised. (By the way, if you don't have great self-esteem, you can boost it by doing a job that's psychologically fulfilling.) Second, the complexity of a person's environment has been repeatedly demonstrated to have beneficial effects on his or her intellectual abilities and sense of self-worth. Essential and important complex work is defined as work that requires thought and independent judgment—and

The high-self-esteem overachiever is confident about her future: She always intended on being hugely successful in her career and in her relationships. And there are more such women in our generation than ever before.

that's what stay-at-home-mom work is all about. (Hey, if running a household weren't challenging, then why would women in the 1950s have needed Valium to get through the day? It was called mother's little helper for a reason.)

Studies have shown that complex household work is associated with greater intellectual flexibility and higher self-esteem in women. The home-maker's role is vital, multifaceted, complex, and challenging. And it can make the stay-at-home mom feel good about herself and her accomplishments. When your eight-year-old comes home with a good grade, you as the over-achieving stay-at-home mom can see how you have positively influenced your child, and nothing—nothing—can make you feel better about who you are. Es-pecially given the complexities of trying to run a smooth household: Your six-year-old has had a terrible ear infection for several days; the water heater is on the fritz; the kids are worried about their hamster, who isn't his usual perky self and needs to go to the vet; you need to get your ten-year-old off to her sax-ophone lesson; and you have to make something for dinner, taking your eight-year-old's egg allergy and your ten-year-old's wheat allergy into consideration. Kids are unpredictable, life is unpredictable, and it's your job to make every-thing as predictable for them as possible. Nothing is as complex as that.

The Mastery Mindset

Women who have a good sense of self-worth tend to be less daunted by the challenges that life throws in their path. No one gets an easy ride: Some of the most famous people faced setback after setback. Think of the phenomenally successful author J. K. Rowling, whose first Harry Potter book was rejected by publisher after publisher until someone had the sense to see just how good it was.

High-self-esteem overachievers face setbacks just like everybody else, but they're like the Energizer Bunny: They just keep going. A healthy sense of self gives a woman the strength to withstand a setback. Strong self-esteem means you don't feel defeated and give up, deciding to sit on the sofa with a box of Cheetos instead. This is what makes high-self-esteem overachievers tick: When they suffer a setback, they're strong enough not to give in to fears about their own self-worth and ability. Instead, they focus their energies on finding another way to reach their goal. They don't quit; they keep on overachieving and striving for perfection.

If you have a healthy sense of self-esteem, you are less likely to spend time thinking self-deprecating thoughts—e.g., *I failed because I'm worthless*—and more time improving the skills you need to succeed at your goal on your next attempt. In psychological terms, this is called *using mastery as a technique to maintain self-worth*. Mastery is when you decide that the way to achieve your goals is to become the most competent person you possibly can be. You develop as much knowledge as you can so that little is left up to chance: You get really, really good at something. Francesca works in computing and has learned everything there is to know about the software that she works with, and beyond. "I don't want to be in a situation, especially as a woman, where I don't know something about my field," she says. "It gives me job security. My boss knows that I am the go-to gal with anything and everything in software. I wouldn't have it any other way, especially when I know that there is a management position opening up. I'm a shoo-in and it's because of how much I know and how hard I have worked, but I am also willing to learn. There is new technology coming out every day and I am completely open to learning all that I can."

Psychologists will tell you that Francesca will likely achieve her goals because she is willing to keep a learning perspective. Self-esteem really comes to the fore when women like Francesca fail. It has been shown that mastery-oriented overachievers don't waste time thinking they are inherently incapable or lacking in worth; instead, they explain failure in terms of lack of effort. They will say, "I didn't do my best" or "I didn't try as hard as I could have" and resolve to make more of an effort next time around.

> Mastery-oriented overachievers don't waste time thinking they are inherently incapable or lacking in worth; instead, they explain failure in terms of lack of effort. They will say, "I didn't do my best" or "I didn't try as hard as I could have" and resolve to make more of an effort next time around.

They look at where they need to improve their skills and knowledge, then come back for another bite of the apple. The research supports this: One study found that women who were mastery-oriented spent all of their time after a failed attempt trying to really understand the task—the how, the why, the inner workings of it—and they tried to learn as much as they could about it. Interestingly, they were more focused on the act of learning about the task than on worrying about whether they were likely to fail on the second attempt. Non-overachievers spent all of their time figuring out ways to not fail rather than ways to learn, and their chance of

to do   Change the Way You View Failure

Many of us were raised to believe that if we fail at something, we are failures; that it's a black-or-white situation. Nothing could be further from the truth. One failure does not a future make, but instead a chance to learn what went wrong. Take Milton Hershey, for example. I'm guessing that you have heard of Hershey's chocolate and that once a month you may even keep Hormone-zilla at bay with an offering of a Hershey's kiss or two. Well, did you know that before he started the Hershey's Food Corporation, sweet Milton started not one but four candy companies that failed miserably and forced him to file for bankruptcy? He wasn't alone: Henry Ford's first two automobile companies failed and at the age of forty, with a bank balance of just under $224, he tried again—and you can see how that all turned out for him. Take a page from Hershey's and Ford's book and learn that with great failure can indeed come great reward. You have to believe in yourself despite what others may say to you or what your fears tell you. You can't see the whole parade from where you stand, so you have to keep striving and trust that one day you'll be living your dream.

failure a second time was greater. This mastery mindset—which leads to the kind of successes that are like oxygen for overachievers—comes more naturally to women with good self-esteem. And it nourishes their self-esteem, too: It's a cycle.

High Self-Esteem and Decision-Making

Strong self-esteem plays another significant role in overachieving behavior: It influences the kinds of decisions a woman makes, and her ability to stick to them. A woman with strong self-esteem feels that her decisions matter, so she is more likely than her sisters with lower self-esteem to make decisions that lead to personal success.

Here's an example: Charlene is offered a promotion at work. Her self-esteem is not the strongest and so the offer brings up questions such as: *Do I really have the skills to do this? What if I fail? This new job will mean long hours: Will my relationship with my husband suffer? What if I end up divorced?* She agonizes over whether to take it or not, and after much soul-searching she goes back to her boss a week and a half later and says yes, she's up for the challenge. Too late: Her boss has already moved on and offered it to Janet, a quintessential overachiever, who accepted the job immediately. Janet has a pretty strong sense of self-worth. Her thought pattern went more like: *This promotion is an acknowledgment of how valuable I am. I'm not as experienced as Charlene, but I can master the skills I need. I'll have to work late a lot, but my husband loves me and appreciates me for who I am, so he'll understand. I'll balance it all.* In cases like this, strong self-esteem means that an overachieving woman is more likely to make a decision that leads to her own advancement—and thus end up with something else to add to her list of successes.

The Influence of Poor Self-Esteem

We were all born with unique personalities and grew up in various environments, exposed to different life events. All these things affect our self-esteem too. While women generally have experienced decades of social change leading to increased opportunities and a greater sense of self-confidence and self-worth, individually some of us do have self-esteem issues. These issues are a less positive motivation for overachieving, which makes them perhaps even more important to understand.

In Chapter 5, I briefly talked about women who strive for perfection as a way of masking the fact that deep down they feel pretty negative about themselves. For these women, having a packed schedule, a résumé bursting with achievements, an immaculate appearance, and a perfect home could be a way of having something they can point to, as if to say: "See, I do have value, I do have worth. Look what I can do!"

Some women become overachievers because they have a strong urge to prove the doubters (including themselves) wrong. Kathy is a great example of this. She has a busy job, three kids, is the president of a local community charity, and every moment she gets she's out running and training at the gym. She has a goal: to finally finish the marathon in her city. Last year she nearly made it but she had to walk the last mile.

Her overachieving started back in junior high, when she was more of a bookworm than an athlete. Two things happened at a very important time in her development that shook her sense of self-worth. The first disappointment was taking second place in a big spelling bee. To this day, she can still see the look on Mrs. Browne's face when she failed to correctly spell her last word: *officious*. In many schools, teachers do double duty—for me, it was my earth science teacher, who was also my softball coach. For Kathy, it was Mrs. Browne, who was her gym teacher as well as the academic club coach. So Mrs. Browne knew Kathy's limitations both as a speller and as an athlete.

Her humiliating moment—missing the word at the spelling bee—became a symbol for her inability to really achieve; a metaphor of sorts. Now Mrs. Browne was her icon for failure.

The second event that had a big influence on Kathy occurred in her gym class. Kathy was running around the field and Mrs. Browne said to her (probably—okay, maybe—in jest), "Oh, in your own time, Kathy. We have nothing better to do than watch you!" When Kathy heard some of the kids laughing at her, her face turned red, just like it had at the spelling bee. It was "officious" all over again. But it was worse now, as she melded the two experiences—the two moments of humiliation—in her mind as one.

These events affected Kathy's self-esteem, but in true overachiever style, she didn't let them deter her. She responded by working harder and achieving more. She started running regularly, with the goal of completing a marathon. While Kathy has never been athletic, she is driven to triumph over these negative experiences and unconstructive memories.

Kathy envisions herself crossing the finish line, and it looks something like this: It's that last mile marker; she feels her body about to fail her but she knows that she has what it takes to complete this marathon now; she isn't that little girl anymore. She can reach her goal: She's trained, she's eaten right, and she's worked

to do   Overcoming Humiliating Moments

If you are plagued by memories of humiliating moments from your past, there are three ways to put them behind you and move on:

Appreciate them. You can work your whole life to create the perfect image, but it's those flawed moments that stand out as a testing ground for your character. Do you know the saying "What does not kill me makes me stronger"? Well, a similar principle applies. The humiliating moments of your life can be pivotal events that give you the chance to grow stronger and define yourself to the world.

Embrace them. Wear them like a badge of honor and learn to love the imperfection and the humanness you now possess. If you embrace embarrassment you defuse it, just as you stop a bully in his tracks by standing up to him. Don't let these memories bully you by making them mean more than they really do.

Share them. You think you're the only one who's had humiliating moments in her life? Every woman has been in similar, if not worse, situations. When you begin to share your stories you'll see how mistakes, goof-ups, and embarrassing moments are a rite of passage for all of us. (You may even find that your own pale in comparison!)

hard. Finally, as she crosses the finish line she throws her arms in the air and falls to her aching knees, yelling "Officious: Volunteering one's services when they are not asked for or needed. O—F—F—I—C—I—O—U—S. *In your face, Mrs. Browne!*"

On the other hand, some women with a shaky foundation of self-worth look to pleasing others as a way of feeling better about themselves. This is the kind of harried overachiever who doesn't stop for a second because she's always doing something for someone else—a friend, a family member, a colleague, a local community group, the next-door neighbor, a woman she met at the grocery store who looked like she was having a bad day . . . . These women constantly give of themselves to others and take nothing in return. They have no "me time" because they live to be of service to everyone else.

If you *are* this woman, ask yourself this: Am I in fact sending a message to my friends, family, and colleagues that I don't matter? Do I feel, deep down, that I can only earn love by doing things for others? Self-esteem has a very large component of self-respect to it. Women with self-respect say "no" all the time, because they realize that their own personal goals and desires are important too.

Overachievers with a less-than-robust sense of self-esteem have learned that the accolades they receive for their achievements make them feel good about themselves. And who doesn't want that? Let's say you put a huge amount of effort into making your home look perfect. You spend every spare moment touching up paintwork, shining windows, digging flower beds, trimming hedges. Neighbors start to compliment you on how beautiful it looks; it makes you feel

Read the following statements and circle "yes" or "no":

1. I can't bring myself to correct others, even when I know they're wrong.
   Yes / No

2. There are things on my to-do list that I don't want to do but have agreed to do for other people because I'd feel guilty otherwise.
   Yes / No

3. When I deserve something such as a promotion or a break, I find it very hard to ask for it.
   Yes / No

4. I resent at least one person who is close to me because I feel he or she takes advantage of me, yet I dare not discuss it with that person.
   Yes / No

5. I regularly do more for others than they do for me.
   Yes / No

6. It makes me feel superior when I do things that please others.
   Yes / No

7. I avoid confrontation at all costs.
   Yes / No

8. I feel more threatened than most people do when someone is overly assertive or aggressive.
   Yes / No

9. I feel drained and angry at the end of most days.
   Yes / No

10. I feel like I get very little support and if it weren't for me, everything would fall to pieces.
    Yes / No

If you answered "yes" to four or more questions on this list, then you are somewhere between an overachiever and a doormat. It's time that you learned your worth and started saying "no" more often! Each time someone asks you to add another chore to your to-do list that benefits him or her, not you, ask yourself whether that person will do the same for you sometime in the future. You should only give to those people who you know will do the same for you. Of course, there are some relationships where you will inevitably do more—with your children, especially when they are young, or your parents when they are very elderly, for example. But when it comes to your fit and healthy adult peers, the relationship should be equal. You need to start saying "no" to people who don't reciprocate. You also need to stop going out of your way for people who don't respect your time and how busy you are.

How to Say "No" with Grace

How do you all of a sudden start saying "no"? With elegance and style, that's how. Here are some tips.

- Let everyone know that you're busy taking care of your own responsibilities. You don't need to give detailed excuses: A simple "I'm swamped right now" is all it takes.

- If your boss wants to lay some more work on you, it's okay to say that you need to limit the amount you take on to prevent your work from suffering. "I'm prioritizing quality over quantity and it's working better for me" is something you can say that is hard to argue against. What is your boss going to say: "No, I want you to do crappy work and lots of it"?

- Flip it back onto them! The next time someone tries to add something of his or her own to your to-do list, say, "I'm confident that you will do a wonderful job with this all on your own." It will reassure that person that he or she is capable, that you respect him or her, and that you have faith in his or her abilities. It's a way of standing up for yourself without bruising anyone's ego.

- Social obligations can be especially hard to say "no" to. You don't want to be dismissive and end friendships, so if you're feeling overwhelmed and overscheduled and just can't face that dinner or coffee, be warm and open. Tell your friends how much you appreciate their friendship, but that you have been so busy that tonight you have to take some personal time to recharge your batteries. They'll get it.

- "No" is usually harder to say than it is to hear. You'll be surprised at how well most people accept a tactful "no." It creates more anxiety for you than it does for the other person. Once you've done it a few times, you'll see that most times, when you say a polite "no," people just say "okay." You'll begin to feel more in control.

good about yourself. No, you feel *great*. Your time in the garden gets you interested in landscaping, so you enroll in a landscape design course a couple of nights a week after work. You submit your first assignment and you get an *A* for it—that gives you even more of a boost. You manage to squeeze in helping out at your son's school bake sale. It's a pretty disorganized operation, but you get things running smoothly. The principal herself asks you to head the bake sale committee and you agree, feeling appreciated and worthy. Another overachiever gets her wings!

to do You're Worth More

Here's a great way to discover that you're so much more than your achievements: List the aspects of your personality that combine to make you one of a kind and make you feel good about yourself. You can include any special talents you possess—so long as they don't have anything to do with your résumé! Don't stop until you have come up with at least ten. Here's the list of a woman who is a partner at a law firm:

- I have a great sense of humor.
- I am a loving person.
- I can do math really well, in my head, without a calculator.
- I am an excellent artist.
- I'm a very loyal friend.
- I have a strong grasp of politics.
- I do my bit to look after the environment.
- I have a strong sense of spirituality.
- I know good music.
- My chocolate-chip pancakes could win awards.

If this describes your life, don't forget that you are more than the sum of your achievements. Making your sense of self-worth contingent upon your achievements works great—until your hedge inexplicably turns brown, your teacher criticizes your latest landscape design, and the bake sale committee's accounts won't balance. A crucial element of good self-esteem is that it remains constant no matter what happens in your life. A strong, unshakeable sense of self means that in the face of adversity, you know who you are and you can bounce back. While your achievements make an important contribution to your sense of self, there is so much more to you, and you need to remember that when things don't turn out as you had planned.

> While your achievements make an important contribution to your sense of self, there is so much more to you, and you need to remember that when things don't turn out as you had planned.

Faux-verachievers

"If I see one more ribbon or trophy that says 'Great job just for being on the team' being dragged in by my daughter Mya, who once again sat on the sidelines, I am going to scream so loud that I will break the crystal vase that she got for just showing up at last year's debate club," Jenna groans.

Jenna is the mother of ten-year-old Mya and nineteen-year-old Allison, and she has highlighted a very real problem: High self-esteem built upon a flimsy foundation. I'm all for faux—on the collars of jackets. What worries me is when I see faux self-esteem being instilled in young women. The motivation behind the awards and trophies that Jenna mentioned is a good-hearted one, but Jenna says that the contrived self-esteem-building has not helped her daughters. She feels that they don't have the drive and ambition that she had when she was their age. As a matter of fact, Jenna believes that all the feel-good accolades they've received have had the opposite effect. Allison, who is in her second year of college, is having a rough time because she actually has to do the work and no longer receives praise just for showing up. "Allison is finally being challenged and she is failing at some of her subjects, and it scares me that it will crush her to the point where she will just stop trying," says Jenna. "Being unprepared is having the opposite impact on her self-esteem."

In addition, these self-esteem-building techniques may be influencing the current generation of young adults to be more self-absorbed and narcissistic than ever before. *Narcissism* is defined as a pervasive pattern of grandiosity characterized by arrogance, an overall feeling of entitlement, and a lack of empathy and concern for others. Two rock stars in the world of psychology, Jean Twenge and Keith Campbell, came out with a pivotal study in 2007 after interviewing 16,475 college students nationwide over a fourteen-year period, using one of the best survey tools we have, the Narcissistic Personality Inventory. The survey asks participants to endorse or reject statements such as: *People always seem to recognize my authority; I wish somebody would someday write my biography; I find it easy to manipulate people;* and *If I ruled the world, it would be a better place.* What they found was shocking: Two-thirds of the kids fell into the narcissistic, self-centered category. If you're a parent, the take-home message here, which was noted in the study's findings, is that expectations of what your kids can achieve have risen just as the world is becoming more competitive, creating an enormous clash between expectations and reality, and thus greater levels of narcissism in children. Narcissistic kids tend to react aggressively to criticism, lack real coping skills, don't believe they should have to work hard, and can't take rejection well—and learning to do all of these things is imperative for achievement, let alone overachievement.

The educators and community leaders who tried to build up Mya's and Allison's self-esteem probably thought they were helping them to avoid developing unstable self-worth, but instead of giving them real skills, they gave them rewards and awards they didn't earn. There is something to be said for a girl having some autonomy over her own life, and the chance to make decisions for herself, even if it means she fails sometimes. Failure can be used as a motivator. Thinking that failure is bad for a kid is a mistake: Failure is an enormous character and self-esteem builder; if a girl is allowed to fail, she will have to learn both coping skills and problem solving, making her feel competent.

> There is something to be said for a girl having some autonomy over her own life, even if it means she fails sometimes.

As a matter of fact, a 2007 study by researchers at The City University in London found that girls who modeled were less happy than other girls their age. One possible explanation: They were not allowed to fail, nor were they allowed to make decisions for themselves, thus they didn't develop any competence. The development of competence has a strong link to self-esteem-building, and it is significant for a developing teen girl. Self-worth that fluctuates wildly, depending on the kind of day you're having, is not healthy. No one wants self-esteem that is fragile and changes from one day to the next. Well, ironically, a lot of these faux self-esteem-building activities that your kids are involved in are creating just that. I have some more news: It's true for you too. "Just feel good" superficial self-esteem boosters that are grounded in nothing aren't helping any of us.

> It's great that more and more people understand the need for a positive self-image, but that image must be based on something real and solid. Because, let's face it, reality will come up to bite you every time.

The message here is that true self-esteem—the kind that is strong enough to withstand the trials of life, especially the life of an overachiever—needs a solid foundation. It's great that more and more people understand the need for a positive self-image, but that image must be based on something real and solid. Because, let's face it, reality will come up to bite you every time. Instead of focusing on the kind of "just feel good" superficial self-esteem boosts Jenna mentioned, we should be developing real self-esteem. And that means a bit of hard work, not just showing up. Look to the example set by the most successful of women, who know that the path to success is mastery (honing the skills you need to reach your chosen goal), the ability to see failure as a learning opportunity and come back to try again, and, of course, the key to it all: self-acceptance.

You're in Control

If you could live your entire life basking in the glow of strong self-esteem, you would have few conflicts and concerns. But I hate to tell you that many of us are a bit more complicated than that. We have our good days and our bad days. And you may feel differently about yourself in different arenas. There are many areas in which you know you excel, so you feel great about who you are when you are in those situations. Yet there may be other areas where you are out of your element and don't feel as confident about asserting yourself.

Earlier in the book we touched on the idea of your *global sense of self-worth:* the totality of how you feel about yourself based on how you see yourself (self-appraisals), how others really see you (actual appraisals), and how you think others see you (reflective appraisals). Your self-appraisal—how you see yourself—changes depending on how comfortable and confident you feel in a particular environment. Therefore, your global sense of self-worth can fluctuate. That's why it's important to develop ways to stay in control.

So how *do* you raise self-esteem? Unconditional self-acceptance. This means learning to accept who you are no matter what environment you're in, no matter how bad a day you're having, and no matter what others are thinking or saying about you. The only way that you can accomplish all of your goals is to hold on to who you are—and that includes the bad stuff too. Having a crummy day or bombing at something once in a while not only makes you human, it makes you, *you*.

to do — Tips for Raising Self-Esteem

See failure as an opportunity. When something goes wrong, learning to see failure as an opportunity to develop new skills and strategies will not only help you succeed at reaching your goals but will protect your self-esteem too.

Accept love and support. Receiving love and support helps your self-esteem, so if you are having a crappy day, call someone who loves you. And when she tells you how much she loves, admires, and appreciates you, believe her.

Accentuate the positive. Hanging around with negative people who reinforce your negative self-talk is only going to drag you down, but surrounding yourself with positive people will give you a self-esteem boost. Everyone has a friend or two like this—you know, the ones who never fail to make you smile and feel good about yourself and the future. Go have coffee together, or invite them over for dinner.

Work it out. There is no question that exercise makes you feel better. It causes the release of the feel-good brain chemicals known as endorphins and makes you feel more positive because you know that you've done

The most successful women are the ones who accept rejection and failure and don't get crippled by them, because they have unconditional self-acceptance. The idea is to keep yourself as grounded as possible and retain your sense of self in any environment, no matter what people are thinking about you or what you *think* they're thinking about you.

> The idea is to keep yourself as grounded as possible and retain your sense of self in any environment, no matter what people are thinking about you or what you *think* they're thinking about you.

something to care for yourself and your health. No matter how hard it seems, when you are feeling low, get out and do something, even if it's just a ten-minute walk around the block.

Do something you're good at. When you are in a self-esteem slump, do something that you enjoy and that you feel confident about doing. It could be swimming, knitting, solving sudoku puzzles, or playing solitaire—just make sure it's something fun that will give you a sense of achievement.

Be open-minded. When your self-esteem is low, it's like an old scratched record playing the same thing over and over in your head. You know what? Maybe that self-doubting voice is wrong. Keep your mind open; you may learn something new that changes your opinions about lots of things, including your opinion of you.

Volunteer. I know you've got a lot in your schedule, but even a small amount of volunteer work for a community cause gives a huge boost to your self-esteem. Helping other people, looking after the environment, protecting the welfare of animals—any of these things will remind you that you play an important role in the world and are valued and appreciated.

Chapter Ten

Life Events as Triggers for Overachieving

*A sudden or even tragic change to the status quo
can have an unexpected consequence:
It can inspire you to achieve more.*

Life, as they say, is full of surprises. Some of us live with daily drama and even go looking for it, while others enjoy the steady murmur of life in idle. Either way, an unexpected event can take hold of your world and turn it upside down in a second.

I've established that many overachievers are compelled by failure to hone their skills, try even harder, and move forward rather than to stumble, and that they have a unique ability to see a setback as an opportunity to learn. When an ordinary woman experiences a major life event, she can suddenly discover this same quality within herself, and her inner overachiever is unleashed.

Take Leanne Preston, an Australian woman who heads a multi-million-dollar company that makes natural health care products for children. She left school when she was fifteen, married when she was in her early twenties, and gave up work in order to raise three children. When her relationship with her husband ended, she suddenly found herself a single mom without a roof over her head and living on welfare; she even spent some time with the kids in a women's shelter. She was devastated and at first she felt like just giving up.

to do   Find the Positives

How do you become the type of woman who can turn a negative life event into an opportunity to create something positive? Here are some tips.

Have a "can-do" attitude. If you take action instead of being passive, and if you stay strong so that nothing will sway you from your course, you will have a much greater chance of achieving something positive after a crisis. Believing that you can do something is half the trick of actually doing it.

Complain effectively. After a negative life event you'll need to express your feelings, and you may feel that you have a lot to complain about. There are effective ways to complain—for example, sharing your feelings with a friend and discussing what your options are, or lobbying Congress for a reform that will spare other women from suffering whatever you've been through. And then there are ways to complain that will just drag you down—for instance, whining to anyone who'll listen about how bad things are but not actually taking any action.

After her divorce settlement she received a small amount of money—enough for a down payment on a house for herself and the kids. She had a part-time job by then and would have just been able to make the mortgage payments. But, with her children's support, she parlayed the money into a risky but exciting venture: starting her own company. She had no formal business training or experience running a company and certainly didn't have a chemistry degree, but driven by a belief in the importance of children's health, she started formulating her own natural products at her kitchen

Work hard. After the initial period of coping with the shock of a negative life event, it's time for some hard work. I wish it were possible to wave a magic wand, but there really is no other option. Look at it this way: Every bit of work you do gets you closer to your goal, and being busy helps you stop dwelling on the negatives of your situation.

Define what positive means to you. Don't automatically accept society's version of what a negative life event is; otherwise you run the risk of wallowing in self-pity. Society around you may see the event you have lived through as wholly negative, but no situation is entirely black or entirely white. You have to be a survivor, you have to move on, and that means seeing the glimmer of hope in even the most negative situation. Be open. When things get too tough, talk to a friend or seek counseling. And be open to the idea that misfortune can bring about great things.

sink, using essential oils in place of the toxic chemicals other companies used. She worked night and day, seven days a week to establish her business, and even pored over scientific papers at her local library to learn everything she needed to know. Ten years later her business is booming, her products are sold all over the world, and she is even involved in developing a way to stop the spread of malaria, an endeavor that could save the lives of hundreds of thousands of children a year.

Your Response to a Life Event
Attitude

Researchers have found that people are unique in the way they handle major life events. Two women who face the same life event will have two different reactions, will make different decisions about what to do next, and will perceive the gains and losses of the situation differently. When you experience a stressful life event, you have to make certain adjustments: You have to adapt to the new situation. Some women have the capacity to bend, while others crumble under the pressure. Your underlying attitude is the key: In the face of a stressful life event, do you feel helpless, or do you feel that you still have some control over what happens to you?

The woman who feels helpless tends to explain the cause of a negative life event in a more pessimistic way than her "I'm in control" sister. In psychological terms, she sees the cause of a negative event as *internal and stable*. This is a fancy way of saying that she blames herself—she internalizes the situation—and sees it as a fixed and unchangeable problem. For instance, if her company downsizes and she loses her job, she might think: *I got laid off because I'm not smart enough, and I will never be smart enough.* When something good happens to her, she views the cause in the opposite way, as *external and unstable.* For instance, if she gets a promotion she thinks *Whew, I got lucky!* This kind of outlook doesn't lead to a life of overachievement. In fact, this more pessimistic woman is at risk of being an underachiever, as well as of developing a whole slew of depressive symptoms.

> In the face of a stressful life event, do you feel helpless, or do you feel that you still have some control over what happens to you?

Women who feel that they do have control over their world don't blame themselves for negative life events, and they don't believe that good outcomes are all about luck and happy accidents. They respond to a negative life event by searching for an opportunity to make something positive from it.

There are many stories of women who have turned terrible tragedy into major triumph. Representative Carolyn McCarthy comes to mind. In 1993 her husband was killed and her son critically wounded on a Long Island train by a disturbed man with a gun. All told, six people died and the gunman would have killed more had he not been wrestled to the ground by some brave folks. Carolyn did something brave, too, and amazing and inspiring considering her loss:

She transformed herself from homemaker and nurse to gun-control advocate and Democratic candidate for Congress. An incredibly smart and strong woman, she was more than a one-issue candidate and she won a seat in the House of Representatives, beating the lackluster incumbent. She is an inspiring example of how a woman can achieve great things as a result of a major—and even tragic—life change.

to do · Expand Your Social Network

If you feel that your social network is in need of expansion, it's time to get out there and mingle. Here are some pointers.

Take rejection in stride. Not everyone you approach at a social event is looking for a new gal pal, so don't take it personally.

Use work activities or kid-related activities to bond. It's perfectly okay to suggest lunch or a coffee sometime if you happen to hit it off with someone you meet at a conference for work or your baby's play group.

Join stuff. Book groups are great places to make new friends. So are gym classes, volunteer organizations, or any other group where people share the same interests or occupation as you.

Be proactive. Start a group yourself. Get a weekly dinner together every Saturday for women in banking, or a Wednesday afternoon lunch for new moms. There are other women out there who would love to talk about the same things as you—just put them together in a room, add some cocktails, and voilà.

Ask around. There's no shame in asking your friends to introduce you to their friends.

Open up. Sometimes it's easy to clam up when you're in a new group of people, but fight that tendency because the more open you are, the more likely it is you will make a friend.

Social Factors

Another factor that determines how you respond to a major life event is your level of social dependence. Do you have a good social support system that you know you can rely upon should something go wrong in your life? Try to imagine receiving some unexpected and unwelcome news: Are there people you can pick up the phone and call who'll meet you for coffee and a chat? Do you have a network of friends and family who can give you advice, support, a hug, a hot dinner . . . a stiff drink? If you do, you're in a much better position to bounce back from a negative life event than your less socially connected sisters.

The size of your social network isn't the only social factor to consider. Also ask yourself this question: Do I let what people think about me define me? Am I in constant need of their approval? If you answered "yes," then that makes you more vulnerable to negative life events. You need the support of friends, family, coworkers, and neighbors—what you *don't* need is to make life choices based on their judgments. If you live and die by what people think of you, then when something goes wrong you may find yourself motivated by fear or shame, rather than by the urge to create something positive.

Stacey and her husband were very wealthy and lived a privileged life in one of the most prominent towns in Connecticut. She had female acquaintances she played tennis with, organized charity events with, hosted dinner parties for. But when her husband's multimillion-dollar business went bankrupt she couldn't bear to face any of her friends or neighbors for fear of their judgments. What would the people of this oh-so-nice town think when Stacey and her husband could no longer afford to pay their country club fees or send their children to camp? Stacey didn't even put her social network to the test: She was so caught up in worrying about what people thought of her that she pulled her children out of the private school they'd been attending for most of

How Reliant Are You on Others' Judgments?

For each of the following, circle A or B.

1. When your best friend expresses a negative opinion about a relationship that you're in, you:

A) Listen, but take it with a grain of salt because only you know what's really going on.

B) Think that she may know something you don't know, and worry that your relationship is in trouble.

2. Your boss isn't happy with the financial report you turned in, so you:

A) Let her know that you only reported what you found and if she isn't happy maybe she should be discussing the business and not your report.

B) Worry that you did something wrong and that she may no longer be on your side.

3. You are waiting in line to pay for a dress at a department store when the woman behind you gives you a look of displeasure. You assume:

A) She's having a bad day and the look on her face has nothing to do with you.

B) It's her way of telling you that the dress would not suit you and you should rethink the purchase.

4. When you have a very important decision to make, you tend to:

A) Look at other decisions you have made that are similar to this, think about how they turned out, and use the information to guide your decision.

B) Ask everyone you know for their opinion and then look at the aggregate of their answers to make your decision—after all, they know you pretty well.

their lives, took them away from the friends they'd grown up with, and basically disappeared to the West Coast.

Another woman might have played it differently. Another woman might have held her head high and chosen not to listen to

---

5. When you receive negative feedback at work, you:

A) Consider it from a business standpoint, but mostly trust that you know what you're doing.

B) Feel very uncomfortable. You hate negative feedback; it keeps you up at night and makes you second-guess your decisions and actions.

3 As (and 2 Bs): You are not overly reliant on others' opinions and are confident. This is a great way to be.

More than 3 As: You are not at all reliant on others' opinions. You are supremely confident, but you should guard against being too bullheaded. If you begin to see a pattern in the negative feedback you're receiving, don't be so quick to think that you cannot learn from it. There's not being vulnerable and then there's being arrogant.

3 or more Bs: You are quite vulnerable to others' judgments and need to learn to trust yourself more. Apply critical thinking to your decision-making: Gather all the facts, compare your options, reflect on how similar decisions have worked out in the past, and then formulate your own decision. Turn to a few trusted confidantes if you're really having trouble, but resist the urge to base your choices on what every Tom, Dick, and Harry thinks. After all, they may not have your best interests at heart the way you, your closest friends, and your family do.

negative judgments—might even have discovered just how many women in her town had lived through a similar experience. When a woman has a good social network but at the same time understands that other people's judgments aren't the be-all end-all, she can make something positive out of a challenging life event. She can go on to work hard and achieve like never before in her life.

Major Life Events

Life can throw all kinds of curveballs at us, and there are as many life events as there are women that they happen to. So let's focus on a few of the more common major life events women face. For some women these life events have an unexpected outcome: revealing the inner overachiever they didn't even know they had.

The Loss of a Partner

Perhaps one of the most stressful—and feared—life changes any of us can face is the sudden loss of our partner. It involves not only grief but also the challenge of getting used to a radically altered way of life. It is a testament to human strength that some women respond to this drastic change not with despair but with hope and courage— and a fresh determination to embrace life.

Carlie, who is in her mid-forties, entered the ranks of over-achieving women relatively late. She had two teenage children and focused on tending to their needs while her husband worked two jobs, both of which he loved. Carlie's life was easy, she says. She wasn't ambitious and had no urge to go out and work; she was content with her life and saw no reason to make any changes. Then one day her husband died unexpectedly, of a heart attack. As you would expect, she went through a period of shock, then grief for the man who had been by her side for almost twenty years.

But soon she found, too, that she was at a crossroads in her life. The financial and emotional support her husband had provided was gone. When her two children went off to college, the reality of her new situation truly hit her. There she was, on her own in the family home, and she couldn't pretend that life would ever be the same again. She had a choice: She could retreat from the world and let life pass her by, or she could make a fresh start. Retreating from the world wasn't going to bring her husband back, and it certainly wasn't going to pay for her kids' education. Carlie went back to school herself to brush up on her skills as a medical administrator, which is what she'd been before she was married. Soon she was going to work every day at a nearby hospital. She is now able to help out with her kids' school expenses. She's continuing to study at night to keep building on her skills, she has become heavily involved in her local cycling club, and when she isn't out on her bike with her new friends she's out in her yard—she's been reading up on organic gardening and is now growing most of her own vegetables.

Katharine Graham is a more high-profile example. She was born to a wealthy family who owned *The Washington Post* and divided their time between homes in New York and Washington, D.C.

Katharine married Phillip Graham, a Harvard Law graduate and clerk to two prominent Supreme Court justices. She gave up her career as a reporter for *The Washington Post*, choosing to raise a family and bolster her husband's booming career instead. After the death of Katharine's father, Phillip became publisher of *The Washington Post* in 1946 and expanded the family's media empire by buying several television stations and the magazine *Newsweek*.

But Phillip led a troubled and tumultuous life. He suffered a nervous breakdown, was diagnosed with bipolar disorder, and admitted to having an affair with a *Newsweek* journalist. He committed suicide in 1963. Now Katharine found herself in control of *The Washington Post* and the rest of the family's media holdings. She had no experience in running a media organization, and many people speculated that Katharine would sell *The Washington Post* and the rest of the family's media empire to someone more experienced, or to a larger company. But that didn't happen. She bounced back from a string of tragic life events, collected her savvy, poise, and her most positive energy, and took the reins of the company. Though she had no female role models who had been publishers before her, she became president of *The Washington Post* and was soon chairman of the board. She went on to employ some of the most powerful men in the country, such as Benjamin Bradlee, Bob Woodward, and Carl Bernstein; presided over the *Post* at the time the paper uncovered the Pentagon Papers and the Watergate scandal; and won a Pulitzer Prize for her memoirs in 1998. On becoming president of *The Washington Post*, she said in her memoir: "What I essentially did was to put one foot in front of the other, shut my eyes and step off the ledge. The surprise was that I landed on my feet."

Divorce

Everyone knows that many marriages end in divorce, yet when you go into a marriage you never think that yours could be one of them. That's why it can be such a shock and a setback when a marriage ends: You dreamed of (and usually worked damn hard to build) a marriage that would last all your days, and you may be mentally and emotionally unprepared for life after divorce. In the months and even years after divorce, you may have a lot of loss to deal with: the loss of what once had been a loving relationship, a lifestyle and routine you were comfortable with, a future you'd envisaged with your partner, a shared home filled with memories, and even your sense of hope. Add possible feelings of failure and guilt—and for those with children, concern about the pain divorce might cause the kids—and you have a potent cocktail of negative emotions.

On top of the emotional impact of divorce there are financial issues too. When you're planning a wedding you're usually wondering about things like whether it's okay to make your best girlfriends wear those aubergine taffeta bridesmaids dresses you've dreamed of since you were eight, rather than what you'll do if you end up as a divorce statistic. Yet after divorce many women find themselves in a vulnerable situation because they made personal sacrifices for their marriage and their family that affected their career. If you

Starter Marriages

A starter marriage is one where the couple marries young and gets divorced before the arrival of the first child—and usually before the arrival of the first wrinkle. Starter marriages are more common among overachievers. Women who see themselves as part of a "power couple" are a great example. They are trying to do it all: A fabulous career? Check. A great home in that hip neighborhood? Check. A husband? Check. While there may be a dog involved, there are never children. However, both halves of the couple are too busy to nourish a marriage, and the almost-inevitable outcome is divorce.

Some have said that a starter marriage isn't a bad thing because it's a learning experience, it demonstrates that both parties were capable of a certain level of commitment (albeit not a lifelong one), and it feels more like a breakup with a really good live-in boyfriend than one with a life partner. An overachiever may view her starter marriage not so much as a tragedy but as an opportunity to try again and perfect it next time. Hey, who else but an overachiever would consider a marriage that didn't work out a "do-over"? The do-over is one of our most powerful alternatives: It defies time and space, and is like having our very own time machine. Something didn't work out? Doesn't count; we can start over as if it never happened. For most overachievers the urge to move forward is a potent motivator.

The Impact of Divorce on the Overachiever

I'm not saying that divorce affects overachievers less than other women: Pain is pain. In fact, overachievers can feel an extra level of guilt about divorce. Overachievers can be described many ways—highly motivated, driven, ambitious, conscientious, tireless, determined, multi-skilled—but for some of us that list may not include "easy to be with." Guilt about the impact our overachieving personality may have had on our marriage can be just as devastating as the marriage breakdown itself. Divorce can bring out feelings of failure, and that compounds the guilt.

When it comes to relationships, there's no clear marker that states, "Time to get out." And this raises an issue for a woman if she happens to be the one who decided it was time to end the marriage. She might wrestle with doubts about whether she should have left, or stayed and tried harder to make the marriage work. Take Tina. She agonized about divorcing her husband. Of all the things she fancied herself becoming, a divorced woman was not on the list, and at first she was concerned that she had chosen her overachieving lifestyle and her career over her marriage. It took her some time to be at peace with her decision, but eventually she realized that she had done everything she could to make her life with her husband wonderful.

"I can't blame myself," says Tina. "I was there for our kids; the house was always immaculate; I was a great wife. I may have just married the wrong man, and then it got to the point where we were going around in circles and some-one had to say it: 'This isn't working.'" Tina's decision to divorce had not been a hasty one: She knew that she was good about making changes in her career but not so good at making changes in her relationships, so she did a lot of soul-searching and decided to make a real effort to work on her relationship with her husband. She says, "I tried and he didn't, and I knew I had too much time ahead of me to waste any more of it." Tina identifies herself as an over-achiever, but at the time of her marriage breakdown she did not have a partic-ular goal that she was striving for. "I had no major goal in front of me, but when I got divorced, my whole world opened up. As odd as this is to say, it was the best thing that ever happened to me."

continued on next page

. . . continued from previous page

Many of the overachievers that I interviewed for this book said similar things about being divorced: "He wasn't the right guy, so why mourn something that was bad for me when what I have ahead of me is so much more positive? Why dwell on it when all that it does is keep me in limbo and I want to keep moving forward?" This may be what makes driven, motivated women different: a realistic attitude.

Research has shown that overachieving women are better at dealing with life changes such as divorce because they are better at focusing on building new friendships, taking the opportunity to develop a new skill, and being in touch with their feelings. They are also better at turning negative changes into positive ones. Marnie found that going back to school to get her master's degree after her marriage ended had an unexpected perk: "I met a guy ten years younger and I have never had so much great sex in my life. Even a year later we are still having a blast. I had no idea I would love school this much!"

choose to have children, your career may be disrupted by periods of maternity leave and part-time work, and as many women will testify, it can be hard to find your career niche again. With the loss of your partner's salary, the end of a marriage may also mean the end of a certain measure of financial security. It is unfair but true that, on average, women earn less than men, and women may find themselves struggling to make ends meet on their salary alone—especially when children are involved.

It's no wonder, then, that women often feel like they're falling into a black hole when their marriage ends. But the fact of the matter is that after a period of healing, many women become more active than ever before. In some cases it's a matter of necessity: They have bills to pay, so they need to get a second or even third job, or have to go back to school to improve their qualifications so they can earn more. I'll talk about the challenges these women face in the next chapter.

Some women, on the other hand, are inspired to try new things because they now have extra time or feel lonely on their own. With the death of the old routines of her married life, this woman may discover a whole new sense of freedom. She may find the urge to get out of the house and become involved in community groups, learn new skills, do volunteer work, start her own business, or write a novel—or, like a true overachiever, do all of these things at the same time.

For some women, one of the hardest things about divorce is that it changes their identity. They were happy to be known to the world as married; they liked being able to refer to "my husband." Divorce can shake the very foundations of these women—and ironically, that can be an amazing boon. Forced to leave behind their "married woman" identity, they can be free to discover talents, skills, and interests they barely knew they had. And so out of the wreckage of a marriage, an overachiever may be born . . . hey, she has lost time to make up for.

> If you are like most women, it's not so much the loss of the guy that's devastating, but the loss of the life you had imagined with him.

to do

Getting Over a Breakup

There is a timeline for feeling rotten after a relationship breakup, but each day brings new healing. One of the traps you can fall into after a relationship ends is to lose hope about your relationship future. In breakups some very bitter words tend to get thrown around, and your ex's hurtful words may still be echoing in your brain. You cannot let his opinion of you set the tone for who you are and who you'll become in the future. We are changing and growing all the time, and you (and he) are probably different in many ways from when you met and fell in love. Your first job now, post breakup, is to get to know who you are now.

It may help you to remember that this man you broke up with is only one man out of a big wide world of men. Think back to how you met and you'll realize that things could have been so different. You could have been somewhere else that night and met a completely different guy, or your best girlfriend could have introduced you to a different one of her eligible single male friends. Perhaps you would still be with him. Don't put so much stock in the man you just broke up with. Go and find you, then go find someone new. Be happy that you are alive on this earth and that God, or whatever higher power you believe in, has a plan for you, and this all fits into that plan. Trust is your biggest ally.

Breakups

While it isn't quite on the level of death or divorce, a breakup can still be a painful and potentially life-changing event. If you are like most women, it's not so much the loss of the guy that's devastating, but the loss of the life you had imagined with him: that old Tudor house in the nicer neighborhood, the trips to Italy you two would take, and the four kids you would have—all boys, each playing a different competitive sport. (You had even picked out the names: Kyle for the oldest; then there would be Jack, Oscar, and the little one, Markus.) The loss you're mourning is of the life you envisioned: You have to mourn the loss of that house and those kids, even if they did exist only in your imagination. You need to go through a grieving process—but if there's an overachiever inside you waiting to hatch, you might just find that by the time you've reached the bottom of the box of Kleenex you've also enrolled in a course on real estate investment, bought a do-it-yourself book on how to create your very own Tudor manor, and amassed every travel brochure on Italy ever printed. (Kyle, Jack, Oscar, and Markus will just have to wait a little while longer.)

The Empty Nesters

When children leave home it can be devastating—or liberating, depending on your perspective. For women who focused solely on being a mom, this life event can be particularly significant. You may end up even busier than before, joining the growing ranks of the overachieving empty nesters. You could go back to college, take night courses, and learn how to run a great blog or how to tell a cabernet sauvignon from a merlot. Think of all those years when you wanted to start doing charity work, or get a cool job—well, now is your opportunity to do it. All while rediscovering *you*. You know that $200 that you would normally spend on the kids' back-to-school clothes? Now it's heading straight toward the Send Mom to Paris fund. (Not to be mistaken for the Turn the Family Room into Mom's Home Gym fund.) Oh, you've got plans. And I have a special announcement for the newly empty nested: *You've earned it!* Every bruised elbow and ego you soothed, every soccer match or football game you attended, every time you were not supposed to be the car pool mom but you did it anyway, every runny nose and stomach flu you nursed your kids through—all of these have earned you the right to make the most of this life change and achieve all the things you dreamed of.

You're in Control

Sometimes it can seem that you have no control over your fate: You go to work one day and discover that your company has gone

to do

Coping with an Empty Nest

For some new empty nesters it isn't all belly-dancing classes, wine appreciation, and hosting charity balls. For some it's a time of sadness that feels almost like a breakup, complete with feelings of "I'm not needed anymore." I know of one woman, the CEO of a company, in fact, who was so sad when her last son left for college that she would go into his room to sniff his T-shirts and have a cry. Hey, it happens. If you're struggling with being an empty nester, here is some advice.

- Realize that your kids still need you and always will (and they're just a phone call, or perhaps even a quick drive, away).

bankrupt and you no longer have the job you worked at for five years. A family member is diagnosed with a serious illness. Your son gets a scholarship to study at Oxford and while you're happy for him, you can't help but feel a little sad. When things like this happen they seem out of your control, but you can certainly control how you respond to them. If you have a strong sense of yourself and a good social support system (which you have created, FYI), you can cope with change, whatever the change might be. When you experience a critical life event, you have a choice. You can crumple under

> When you experience a critical life event, you have a choice. You can crumple under the strain of change or you can find inner strength, like the women you met in this chapter.

- Be a lady who lunches! Getting back into a social network can help you remember that you're more than just a mom: You're also a really good friend and someone who's fun to be around. Your friendships are going to be most important at this time.
- Know that you raised your children to leave home and to be amazing, independent, wonderful human beings. You did that: It's such an accomplishment!
- Use this time to fall in love with your husband all over again. There are so many things that having kids stopped you from doing, but now, heck, what are you waiting for?

the strain of change or you can find inner strength, like the women you met in this chapter.

Change can be daunting when we don't feel in control of it. A positive step you can take is making sure that you stay informed and involved in the management of change. When life throws something unexpected in your path, learn everything you can about your options and be active in finding a solution. For instance, if you are diagnosed with breast cancer, find out everything there is to know about the disease and your treatment options. If you lose your job, explore every other employment option, phone every connection you've ever made—and eventually you'll find a way to turn what could have been a crushing situation into an opportunity to achieve even more in your career.

And communicate. Let friends, family, neighbors, and coworkers know that you are dealing with a major change in your life. People aren't mind readers and they don't necessarily know how you're really coping with a major event in your life, so make sure you're explicit about what you're going through and what you're currently feeling. Ask them to help you, just as you have helped them in the past.

Finally, know that nothing is forever. You may be suffering because your marriage has ended or your children have all moved away, but with each passing day the stress and anxiety that surrounds your major life event will lessen. Overachievers, as I've said before, are generally good at seeing the big picture—and while living through a crisis, this ability is very important. Keep a firm grip on your sense of self and a long-term view of your life and you'll be just fine, as you always are.

do

Steps to Take in a Crisis Situation

- **Get a pen and paper.** Write down three things you can do to deal with the crisis. For example, in a financial crisis your options might look like: "Get a second part-time job," "Talk to a financial planner," and "Look at my budget and see where I can cut spending." Writing down your options will help to focus your mind so you can see more clearly what you need to do next.

- **Share your woes.** Reminding yourself that you're not the only person who has experienced a crisis helps to give you perspective. Invite friends over, make some hot chocolate, and ask them how they got through crises. Seeing examples of women who have gone through hardship and come out the other side could be just the boost you need.

- **Sleep on it.** Sometimes a good night's sleep is enough to relax your mind so that in the morning you can figure out what to do next.

- **Accept what can't be changed.** At the heart of any crisis there is inevitably a negative, or at worst tragic, fact that all the wishing in the world will not change. If you refuse to accept a cold, hard reality—a serious injury, bankruptcy, the end of a relationship—you'll simply end up exhausted. Tenacity is a good quality only if the end result is within your control—sometimes you have to let go to move forward.

- **Focus inward.** Once you've dealt with what you need to in the immediate aftermath of a crisis, take time to just be and feel. Focus on your emotional life. This will help you rebuild your strength, and the stronger you are, the better chance you'll have to bounce back from the crisis in the long term.

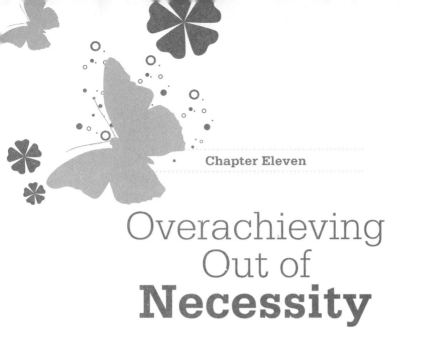

Chapter Eleven

Overachieving
Out of
Necessity

Sheer necessity may drive you to become an overachiever—
and in the process, a real and deep motivation to
reach new goals may grow.

As you've seen already, some women's genetic makeup causes them to want to cook elaborate dinner parties, retile bathrooms, take karate lessons, work two jobs, and get their master's degree in social work, all at the same time. There are other women who become overachievers out of necessity.

My mother, who was a single parent, is a great example of a woman who became an overachiever out of necessity. The latest estimate of how much it costs to raise a child, from birth until the age of eighteen, is just under $200,000. My mother had one child (me), so she only had to raise the two-hundred grand once, but in order to do so she began working and never stopped. She always had a minimum of three jobs. Her main job was as a legal secretary, and she could type like lightning without even looking at the keyboard. (I didn't inherit that skill, so you can imagine how much longer this book took me to write than it would have taken her.) Mom made and sold jewelry as a side business and also ran tennis parties. She thought of everything: While you waited for a court you could play backgammon and socialize. To this day I still have one of her backgammon sets with her tennis-party company name on it, "VSP Parties Limited." Very Special Players, I think. My mother's retired now, but I keep it as a constant reminder of how she took overachieving to a whole new level to give me a good life. And how her legacy lives on.

to do   Cut Credit Card Debt

If you have gotten deep into credit card debt and it's causing problems in your life, it's time to take some action.

- Pay off more than the minimum payment each month, as much as you can spare. If you have multiple credit cards, compare the interest rates and the balances of your cards and focus on paying off the one with the highest interest rate or balance. Make the minimum payment on the remaining cards until you have gotten your first credit card under control. This is the most effective way to reduce your debt, because your debt grows faster the higher the interest rate or balance is.

- Take a good, hard look at what consumer goods you really need as opposed to what you think you need. Do you really need that sweater or whatever item you are considering spending money on?

Types of Necessity

Let's look at some of the major factors that can force a woman to adopt an overachiever's lifestyle out of necessity, such as financial pressure, competition in the workplace, technological change, and lack of support at home.

Financial Pressure

A lot of women in this country find it hard to make it from paycheck to paycheck. Even if you have a partner who works and no kids, two salaries might not seem enough. If you do have kids, well, it's a

- Use credit only in an emergency, when you don't have the money to pay for something but you absolutely need it. (Shoes don't count!) It's simple, really: You should only spend what you have. Living a cash-only lifestyle in a credit-card world is a great way to get your financial life back under control. There isn't a financial expert around who'll tell you to keep revolving credit card debt going. They all tell you to pay it off and never look back.
- This is an old trick, but a good one. Fill a Tupperware container with water, drop your credit card in, and put the lid on. Now put it in the freezer. Having to stand by the kitchen sink waiting for it to defrost will give you enough time to decide whether you really need to make that purchase or not. (Don't get out the hairdryer; that's cheating.)
- If you have multiple credit cards, one can go in the freezer but it's time to cut up the other ones. Go on, it's liberating!

whole other story—especially if you're flying solo. Every month there are utility bills, food, clothing . . . and let's not forget the dreaded debt repayments. High levels of household debt are part of how we live now. Mortgages, second mortgages, credit cards, department store cards, car payments, student loans, personal loans—it seems that almost everyone is swamped with monthly payments. If you have ever-mounting credit card balances and sometimes wake up in the middle of the night wondering if you'll ever manage to pay them off completely, you're not alone. On average 62 percent of Americans are unable to pay off their credit card balances in their entirety. Another sobering statistic: In 2006 more women filed for bankruptcy than graduated from college.

We can't overlook how the high cost of education contributes to debt. You're an overachiever so I don't need to explain to you how important getting an education is. Chances are that you have, at some point in your career, gone back to do some further study. Not only are there tuition fees to pay but you probably had to take out a student loan to make up for all those hours spent hunched over your books instead of out making green. Student loans have a habit of snowballing, especially when you keep adding qualifications to your résumé. Sometimes you find yourself wondering if you'll be sitting on the porch in your rocking chair, still paying off The Fall of the Roman Empire 101.

If you have kids, no doubt you want them to have the same opportunities as you, and then some. Setting aside money for their college fund puts a little more strain on your already over-stretched budget. Increasingly, too, families are paying to put their children through private schools, concerned that public schools aren't giving kids the start they need in life.

Health care takes another big bite out of our budgets. It seems that almost every day on the news someone's talking about the need for reform of the health care system. Millions of Americans have no health insurance at all, making them truly vulnerable if the unthinkable happens and they become seriously ill.

> What has really put a huge dent in our budgets is that our definition of "necessity" seems to be expanding by the day.

Burdened with huge medical expenses, they may even be too sick to keep working, and may find themselves in a downward spiral.

Most Americans do have health insurance, but finding the money to pay for it every month can be a real drain for some families. As an overachiever, you probably look after yourself, stay fit, and eat right, but no matter how hard you try, you could find yourself at the doctor's office. And if you have a health problem that drags on for a while it can be a major, unplanned expense. Add children to the equation and there are seemingly endless visits to the doctor, the dentist, the optometrist, the orthodontist. (Why can't they all be in the same building and at least save you a bit of time?)

Education and health care are two expenses that I'm sure everyone agrees are necessities, much like food on the table and a roof over your head. What has really put a huge dent in our budgets is that our definition of "necessity" seems to be expanding by the day. It now includes things that once would have been considered more science fiction than essential to life on earth. A device that enables you to stand in the dairy aisle of the supermarket and ask your teenage daughter to go look in the fridge at home and see if you need milk? A kind of portable electric typewriter you can take to bed to watch movies, write your blog, or check how your stocks did that day? A gadget that lets you listen to music at the gym while you sweat on an elliptical trainer, which happens to measure your heart rate?

When I think back to what my mother's generation felt they needed versus what our generation feels we need, the difference is astounding. It's not just the electronic gadgets; it's the new clothes we need all the time, the good haircut, the manicure, the gym membership, the decent

Women at Work

Here are some interesting numbers about women's participation in the U.S. labor force from the Women's Bureau of the Department of Labor, 2007.

Almost 60 percent of women ages sixteen and over (69 million out of a total of 117 million) are labor force participants—that means either working or looking for work. That's a lot of women when you take into account how many in that age range are still at school or college.

Almost half of the labor force (46 percent) is made up of women— kind of amazing when you consider how many women take time out of their careers to have children.

The better educated women are, the more likely they are to be labor force participants:

- Less than a high school diploma—32.9 percent
- High school diploma— 53.8 percent
- Some college, no degree— 63.9 percent
- Associate degree— 71.9 percent
- Bachelor's degree and higher—72.9 percent
- Seventy-five percent of working women work full-time, while the remaining 25 percent work part-time.

car, nice housewares, gourmet and organic food every now and then, good wine, dinner out, the pedigree pooch with the adorable little jacket to keep him warm . . . I could go on and on. I'm not about to tell you it's wrong—I'm just making a point that we feel we need a lot more stuff than earlier generations did, and the extra money for all that extra stuff has to come from somewhere.

Add to all of this the fact that the prices of basic items seem to rise way more often than our salaries do (just think of the last time you filled up your gas tank or paid your electric bill) and we have a situation where many women have no choice but to work, work,

Women working in the following employment sectors (expressed as a percentage of all working women):

- Management, professional jobs, and related occupations— 38 percent
- Sales and office occupations— 35 percent
- Service jobs—20 percent
- Production, transportation, and material moving jobs—6 percent
- Natural resources, construction, and maintenance occupations— 1 percent
- Approximately 4 million women (5 percent of all employed women) are self-employed

The top ten money-making occupations for women working full-time and their median weekly earnings:

- Pharmacists $1483
- Chief executives $1413
- Lawyers $1354
- Computer software engineers $1174
- Physicians and surgeons $1134
- Computer and information systems managers $1094
- Medical and health services managers $1026
- Computer programmers $1014
- Physical therapists $1014
- Human resource managers $998

> Many women have no choice but to work, work, work, and then work some more.

work, and then work some more. It might be a case of getting a second job, taking on paid overtime, working extra hard to land a promotion and a pay raise, or studying part-time to improve your earning capacity—any of those things can earn you a place in the ranks of the overachievers.

There's one last factor I'd like to discuss that has made overachieving a financial necessity for some women: the government policy of forcing greater numbers of people off welfare. Regardless of how you feel about the welfare system in this country, it's hard to deny that many women from poorer backgrounds have been raised with little education—and that means fewer job prospects and no expectations.

When the Department of Health and Human Services made it a policy to get people off welfare, these women's only employment options were entry-level, low-paying jobs. They would have to take not one but two, or even three, jobs just to earn enough to survive. Former welfare recipients received training, but often for menial (and therefore low-paying) jobs.

The good in this situation is that many unemployed women got a taste of working and it increased their self-esteem. They decided to get their GEDs or advanced degrees, keep working their way up the ladder, and find better opportunities. They became overachievers without aiming for the label "overachiever" and are an inspiration because they defied the odds.

Competition in the Workplace

The days of joining a company straight out of college and working there forever (or until you got married and had babies and your husband looked after you, à la *Leave It to Beaver*) are long gone. Increasing numbers of women are learning that job stability is an outdated concept. If you've worked for a company that has undergone restructuring, or what is euphemistically referred to as "downsizing" (laying off staff to cut costs), you know what it's like to suddenly be out of a job through no fault of your own. This may have been a blessing in disguise, if you got a good severance package that allowed you to start a business or make some clever investments—but even so, losing your job probably rocked you and left you a little nervous about your future. If you haven't experienced something like this, it might have happened to someone you know and maybe it has you feeling a little edgy too.

While job stability is on the wane, competitiveness in the workplace is on the rise—no doubt the two are related. Perhaps, like many women, you feel there's someone breathing down your neck, wanting your job. Why is it that this person always seems to be younger and hungrier—and *when* did he or she find time to get an MBA? In response to this uncertainty and competition you do what you can to secure your future. First, you make your current job as secure as possible, by being extra-conscientious, putting in extra hours, and taking work home. Second, you build up your résumé so that, should this job end, you'll be in a good position to get another, even better, one. This means studying to improve your credentials, getting involved in industry groups to develop a network of contacts who can help you find a job, and volunteering for projects at work that help you develop new skills. You're leading the life of an overachiever.

Leslie is a great example of this. She was the managing editor of a major publishing company, supervising a staff of ten editors and making sure that about 150 books a year made it into bookstores. "If a book was a day late getting to the printer, my job was on the line. If there was a mistake in a book, my job was on the line," she says. "My boss really pressured me and my colleagues, and there was a culture of fear in the office." To make matters worse, hers was a highly sought-after job and she believed there were plenty of people

to do

How to Survive a Competitive Workplace

- **Stay informed.** Keep up-to-date with developments in your field by subscribing to all the industry magazines and reading all the relevant Web sites and blogs. If there are any big changes in your industry, you need to know about them. Knowledge is power!

- **Refresh your skills.** There are new developments all the time in every industry. Take refresher courses whenever you get a chance.

- **Network.** Join industry clubs if you have to—just get to know as many people in your line of work as you can. They can be a big help when it's time to switch jobs.

- **Stay one step ahead of the game.** Technology and consumer demands change so fast that sometimes entire occupations become obsolete. Always keep your eye out for changes in your industry. If profits are falling for her boss could replace her with. "I would've been content to go to work at 9:00 and leave at 5:30, but I felt this intense pressure to make sure that everything was done perfectly and by the deadline. So I got into work at 7:30 every morning, left around 7:30 at night but took work home, and often worked on the weekend. I didn't have a life outside of work." The interesting thing is that when Leslie eventually changed jobs, she was able to find positives: "That job showed me that I was capable of so much more than I realized. I feel like I can do anything now, that I can achieve anything I set my mind to."

If you have children you may feel additional pressure, because you know that they will one day be facing this competitive environment

years on end or demand for your services is on an ever-downward slide, it might be time to think about retraining for a new career.

- **Keep your perspective.** Are you in a workplace where you and your colleagues feel that your jobs are threatened? Fear is contagious, and once it takes hold it's hard to think about much else. Instead of assuming the worst, try to calmly analyze the situation. Look at the realities from every angle, with a clear head rather than a fearful heart, and you may find that there's no basis for your colleagues' anxiety. However, if your job really does look unstable, don't sit back and wait to see what happens: Call on your network of contacts and start planning your exit strategy.

too. Competition is fierce for places at top colleges, and you want your kids to have the best education and best chance to have great careers. So you may find yourself spending a large chunk of your day prepping your children for the competitive world of adulthood: Driving them around to a multitude of sporting events, music lessons, art or drama classes, or volunteer organizations; helping with their homework or finding them tutors for subjects they're struggling in; being their very own motivational coach. All these extracurricular activities aren't so much a luxury anymore but a necessity to help kids become multi-skilled so they're equipped for the future. Just another few jobs to add to your ever-growing list!

Technological Change

Technology is a wonderful thing that has made life so much easier in so many ways, and saved us a lot of time in the day. Need to know what the sales figures were for December before you can keep going with a report you're writing? Call your sales director on her cell right now and you'll have finished your report before she's back from her meeting with a client. Your bills have to be paid today but you've got meetings booked solidly from sunup to sundown? Go online and have everything paid in a matter of minutes.

Time-saving technology has two sides to it, though. It saves time—but we see the "saved" time as an opportunity to stuff more into our day. Raise your right hand if you think that computers, e-mail, cell phones, and BlackBerries have reduced your workload.

(Nope, didn't think so.) If anything, we seem to be busier than ever before. Natural born overachievers *love* this about technology—it just so happens we've brought quite a few other women along for the ride. They've had to adapt to an overachieving way of life because there isn't much choice: Expectations of what can be done in a day have been raised across the board.

> Time-saving technology has two sides to it, though. It saves time—but we see the "saved" time as an opportunity to stuff more into our day.

Similarly, expectations have been raised for how fast things should be done. We have seen that something *can* be done quickly, so we assume it *will* be done quickly. The sales director whose cell you called for the sales figure you needed to complete your report? How would you feel if you'd gotten her voicemail and she took a little over an hour to call you back? Like many women sweating over a half-finished report due tomorrow morning, you might feel as though this was almost a criminal act on her behalf. The pressure to respond immediately to e-mails and voicemails makes our days very busy: That sales director is still sitting in her car in the parking lot now answering the five other voicemails and three e-mails she received on her BlackBerry while she was in that meeting. (In ads these people are always standing on a scenic bluff at a golf course looking out to sea while they take a call, but that's TV, this is real life.)

The other effect of information technology on our working day is that in many industries, there no longer *is* a working day—it's all one big, long continuum. A lot of us are reachable pretty much 24/7 and the lines between work life and personal life have become blurred. You can answer e-mails on the train. You can answer e-mails while cooking dinner. You can answer e-mails on your laptop in bed. It's not so much that you *can* do these things, it's that you feel you *must* do these things. Women in many professions feel they must be reachable at any hour of the day or night by their boss, staff, or clients. The end result: many more women entering the hard-working world of the overachiever.

to do

Set Limits on Your Working Day

If you're in love with your BlackBerry, you might feel a bit panicky when you hear this suggestion: Have a set time each day that your BlackBerry, work cell phone, and e-mail are turned on, and switch them off the rest of the time. You need at least a few hours each day that you are not working or sleeping. This may drive you crazy at first—let's face it, there's a component of addiction to our reliance on cell phones and BlackBerries—but gradually you will see how great it is to be back in control of your life. You should be the one deciding when work folks can and can't reach you outside of normal business hours, not them. Though you may panic at first that being out of contact will lead to a work-related crisis, soon you'll find that things really can wait. For instance, say you switch on at 8:00 a.m. each day and switch off at 8:00 p.m. The most someone has to wait to contact you is twelve hours overnight—is the world going to come to a grinding halt if they have to wait till the morning? You should, of course, explain to your colleagues or clients that you are setting some limits. They'll soon get used to your new hours of operation, and when they see how much fresher you look, they may even think about setting limits themselves

Lack of Support at Home

The most basic reason that you might need to become an overachiever is that you simply have no support, so everything falls on you. This applies mainly to women who have kids or someone else to look after, say, an elderly parent. Maybe you would really like to delegate some of the things on your daily to-do list but you can't because your household is like a small business, with a staff of just one. You might be a single mom, or perhaps your partner travels a lot for work or works incredibly long hours—either way, you have to do many jobs at once. You're constantly running, from work to day care to band practice to soccer training to the night course you're taking in the hopes you'll get a pay raise . . . to the grocery store to preparing a delicious and nutritionally balanced dinner to doing the laundry to parent-teacher night to scrubbing the bathroom to orthodontist appointments to . . . I've got to stop, I'm getting exhausted.

The life of the caregiver has never been an easy one, but certain social factors have affected our workload in a big way. Increasingly we are having children later in life than earlier generations, and one of the side effects of this is that there may be less support available from our own parents. Grandma and Grandpa can be a big help with kids, but the older you are when you have kids, the older your parents are. They might not have quite enough energy to keep up with your two-year-old, or maybe they've reached a point in life where they need a bit of looking after themselves.

Younger moms might not necessarily have their parents around either. Retirees are not leading the relaxed lifestyles they once did, but are seeing retirement as an opportunity to try new things, travel, relocate, go back to school, get involved in community work, or even start a small business.

Add to this the high cost of child care—and, in some places, long waiting lists for child care—and you have a large pool of women who simply *have* to do it all. And they strive to do it to utmost excellence because they love their kids and they want to give them the best life they can.

to do   You Had Kids, Use 'em!

You may be so accustomed to doing everything at home that even as your children get older and are able to do more, you keep doing all the housework and take full responsibility for organizing their busy lives. You need to learn to gradually give your children more responsibility, appropriate to their age. This means getting them involved in household chores. Start small (for example, getting them to lay out their own clothes for school in the morning when they're young) and build up (allocating them a day of the week on which they have to do the household's laundry when they hit their teens). Get them to start taking charge of their own lives by encouraging them to become more independent and keep track of all the things they have going on—it could be as simple as having their sports gear ready and waiting in their bag for softball practice on Tuesdays so that you don't end up searching under their bed for it. Older kids (at least thirteen years old) can babysit younger ones. Not only will all of this take some of the pressure off you, it will give your children the invaluable lesson of being responsible for others, a strong sense of family, and a great sense of self-worth.

You're in Control

Initially you respond to financial pressures, competition in the workplace, technological change, and lack of support at home in the only way you can: by doing whatever you have to do to get through it. It's a simple survival mechanism. At first it may seem completely out of your control. But know this: When that basic survival mechanism is set in motion, a much more interesting and rewarding process is set in motion too—the process of real self-change. Out of your new life as a very busy woman arises a great desire to transform yourself. Your personality starts to evolve, and you develop a real motivation for achievement, deeper than sheer necessity. And that puts you back in the driver's seat.

> Out of your new life as a very busy woman arises a great desire to transform yourself. Your personality starts to evolve, and you develop a real motivation for achievement, deeper than sheer necessity. And that puts you back in the driver's seat.

How do you know when this is happening to you? You begin to:

1. Express a desire for self-change.

2. Clearly see the difference between the person you were and the person you now want to be.

3. Feel that you may actually, at last, have some control over your own life.

You may have come to it later in life than the natural-born overachievers, but you begin to see that you have goals. And with goals, you can suddenly see the value in things you'd never considered

Tales from the Treadmill: Salma

Salma admits she used to be a slob—her house was a huge mess and the inside of her car wasn't much better. On a regular night she never got to bed before midnight because she was out partying. She was a substitute teacher and when she wasn't called in to work, she didn't do much. When she got married she was happy that her husband had a full-time job and there was no pressure for her to work more. They had their first baby and Salma got a crash course in hard work, early starts, and what it's like to have a job that you can never clock off from. She was exhausted at first, but within two years she had gotten used to it—loved it, in fact—and was ready to have another child. Soon after she got pregnant, her husband began to have back problems. As a manual laborer, he had to cut down on his hours at work, so Salma went back to teaching part-time. She worked right up until a couple of weeks before her baby was due.

By the time their second baby was six months old, Salma's husband had developed serious problems with his knees, as well as his back. He cut his hours even more, so when Salma returned to work she increased her hours a bit. Soon some pain turned into a great deal of pain for her husband and he had to quit work altogether, so Salma got a full-time teaching position.

Salma had to pay all of the bills and the mortgage, and her husband eventually became so incapacitated that over time she began to do everything around the home: the cooking, cleaning, laundry, and even repairs to the house. She now knows how to paint walls and sand floors. As her family's sole provider she couldn't let anything slide at work, so she became extra-involved at school, working late, doing further study at night to expand her skills, and organizing after-school activities for kids. It's been a gradual process; Salma has been forced, bit by bit, to meet the changing needs of her household. She is singlehandedly holding her family together and has become a textbook overachiever, all out of sheer necessity. On the plus side, she feels that being pushed to leave her comfort zone has exposed her to new experiences and a sense of achievement she otherwise wouldn't have had.

before: going back to school to improve your qualifications, actively networking to improve your job prospects, finally starting that small business you've fantasized on and off about since you were in college. . . . You have many hurdles to overcome and it won't be easy—after all, it was sheer necessity that got you to this point, so you aren't exactly on Easy Street. But the payoff when you reach your goals will be sweet indeed.

Conclusion

The reality of being an overachiever is complex. We are all individual women and can't be categorized into a stereotype in the way that shock-horror media stories tend to do. You just read how unique and varied we are, and that there are many different ways to be an overachiever and many different paths to becoming an overachiever. Your overachieving lifestyle may have been encoded into you by genetics; it may have developed in response to the way you were raised as a child, or have been influenced by your sense of self-esteem; or you may have entered the ranks of the overachiever later in life because you had to respond to a crisis, financial hardship, or other unplanned event.

> Overachieving is not a social problem, it is a choice of spirit.

Whichever way you came to the world of the overachiever, I hope this book has shown you that overachieving is a not a disease that needs to be cured. It does not have a negative influence on your happiness, or on how you nurture your children, or your relationships—unless you allow it to. Overachieving is not a social problem, it is a choice of spirit. We live our lives this way because we are naturally predisposed to it or because we live in a world where it is an indispensable quality.

• • •

In addition to my own radio show, I am sometimes a guest on other shows, and one of the questions I've been asked more than once was about self-help books in general, or any book that gives advice and my perspective on it. I think anywhere that you can gain insight into your own life is incredibly valuable. It could be a combination of things that you've read, a poem that touched you, a magazine article, or some advice in this book or any other that gave you pause to take stock of your own motivations and what your life is all about. Because overachievers need to have a strong sense of self to live as we do, we tend to be more introspective, so any insight, any opportunity to look deeper can only be helpful.

Sometimes the greatest insights come from other women sharing their experiences, so I hope that you've been able to take something valuable from the real-life stories of women in this book.

One of my favorite segments from my show is "Bad Day Thursday." It's an opportunity for anyone listening (on a Thursday, of course) to call in and vent about how bad their day was. We give a prize package to the person who had the worst day of all because we'd like to try to end their horrific day with a small token of nice—our wish for the day to not have been a total loss, as well as hopes for a better day tomorrow. Multitasking, overachieving women who usually have it all in balance will call the show to tell stories about how one minor incident sends their seemingly agreeable day cascading into the abyss of *horrendous*. Women who run companies and travel across the country for meetings have called in to tell me and my co-hosts about getting stuck in transit only to miss the meeting that they traveled over 1,000 miles each way to get to, and then having to turn around, come back and pick up children from school—or, in one case, from the principal's office (we suggested bringing doughnuts as a peace offering, which she did).

The story from a woman with two-year-old twins who both had the flu, which kept her up all night caring for them (while her husband slept), was memorable. Finally, after Mom spent a long night taking care of the girls, one toddler eventually went to bed while the other fell asleep on Mom's chest. Morning came and it was time to get up for work, but as she arose, the little girl asleep on her chest also woke up still sick. How did she know? As her eyes opened, the little girl said "Mommy, I don't feel well" and began to throw up, all over her, just as the other twin came running in, covered with, well . . . the runs. Mom scooped up both children and headed for the shower. All three cleaned off and, with moments to spare, Mom handed off the infirm little girls to their daddy, grabbed her shoes, and jumped in the car in her stocking feet. She made it to work just as her meeting was about to begin and threw on her shoes as her assistant set up the Power Point presentation—only to find that her cat had left her a present as well, inside her shoe. Being the pro that she was, she pulled off a stellar presentation, cleaned up as best she could afterward, and made it through the rest of her day. Overachievers can be amazing.

In honor of women like this, I would like to propose a new, politically correct term for women currently labeled "Overachievers." Maybe "Achievement-Oriented Females," or "Active Americans"— something that sends a message to the rest of the world that we choose to live this way and we like it. Achievement gives us meaning and comfort and there is nothing like it.

Acknowledgments

It takes a lot of people to make perfection look easy and I would like to thank everyone who helped me get there, even though I still think I could have done better. Scott Watrous, who has supported and believed in me for many years, my amazingly talented editors Vanessa Mickan-Gramazio and Mary Norris, as well as all of the overachieving women who took time out of their busy schedules to share their stories with me. I am grateful for Nikki Hardin, Inger Forland, and the whole Globe Pequot/skirt! family. Being a woman of achievement, I am aware that it can be a handful for one husband so I have three surrogates to ease his burden: my radio wing-men Anthony Michaels and Chad Bowar, as well as my friend and partner in crime, Kirk Stirland. Special thanks to my hard-working publicists at Susan Blond Inc., Liza, Jaime, and Lisa, and my long-suffering agent Maura Teitelbaum. Oh, and speaking of suffering, I should probably thank my parents Sandi and Bob Durell and my wonderful, supportive, loving husband Sean Lee. I love you all.

About the Author

Cooper Lawrence is a psychology and relationship expert and the host of her own nationally syndicated radio show aptly named *The Cooper Lawrence Show* from Dial Global airing Monday through Friday 7 to 10 p.m. EST. To find a station that carries the show near you or to listen live online, go to www.thecooperlawrenceshow.com.

Cooper holds a master's degree in developmental psychology and is currently finishing her doctorate. She is a regular guest and expert on CNN Headline News's *Showbiz Tonight* and on Fox News Channel's *Live Desk with Martha MacCallum* as well as various shows for the Fox News Channel. She has been seen on *The Today Show, The O'Reilly Factor, The Early Show, Your World with Neil Cavuto, America's Newsroom, Studio B with Shepard Smith, The Morning Show with Mike and Juliet, Fox & Friends, CNN Presents, Nancy Grace, The Insider, The CW11 Morning News* and *The Big Idea with Donny Deutsch.* Cooper has been featured in print for *The New York Post, The New York Daily News, In Style, Cosmopolitan, SELF, Family Circle, Life & Style, Star,* and *US Weekly.*

Cooper is the author of *The Fixer Upper Man: Turn Mr. Maybe into Mr. Right; Been There, Done That, Kept the Jewelry;* and *Cosmo-GIRL's All About Guys.*

She is on the advisory board for *CosmoGIRL! Magazine* where she is The Love Doctor and has also consulted for actress Mariska Hargitay's Joyful Heart Foundation. ✤

Finally, a
skirt!
that fits!

www.skirt.com